TOTAL
SOCCER FITNESS

Ian Jeffreys

ISBN -13: 978-1-58518-051-6
Library of Congress Control Number: 2007926497
Book layout: Deborah Oldenburg
Cover design: Deborah Oldenburg
Text photos: Peter Ashcroft, Powys Sports Academy
Front cover photo: Robert Cianflone/ALLSPORT

Coaches Choice
P.O. Box 1828
Monterey, CA 93942
www.coacheschoice.com

Dedication

This book is dedicated to three very special people:

To my late father, John, who was taken from this world far too soon.

*To my wife, Catherine, and son, James, who make so many sacrifices
to allow me to pursue my passion of strength and conditioning.
You are what makes life so special, and I am blessed
each day to have you both in my life.*

Acknowledgments

This book is the culmination of many years of doing research, attending conferences, talking to coaches, experimenting, and finally integrating various methods into the system outlined in the book. My thanks to all the friends, coaches, and athletes who have helped this development along the way. My great thanks to Daniel Green and Kristi Huelsing at Coaches Choice for their support and hard work in the production of this book. My thanks also to Peter Ashcroft, assistant strength coach at the Powys Sports Academy at Coleg Powys for his help in producing the photographs.

My heartfelt thanks to my father and mother, who instilled in me a passion for learning and sports, without which I would not have been able to pursue this great profession.

My greatest thanks are to my wife, Catherine, and son, James, two very special people. Without their support this text would not have been possible.

Contents

Introduction

As players in all sports become bigger, faster, and stronger, it is becoming increasingly clear that talent alone is simply not enough to get to the top. Optimum performance will only be realized when hard work is allied with talent, and training programs are followed that address every aspect of elite performance. Conditioning is one of the key areas in developing top performers and must be a part of any training program. The beauty of conditioning is that it is completely within an athlete's control, and by following scientifically based programs, all athletes can enhance their conditioning level. An effective conditioning program is clearly a must for developing the modern-day player, and the program must provide multidimensional stimuli to address all of the key fitness requirements of the game.

In terms of analyzing performance, soccer is one of the most challenging games in the world; it requires skill, tactical awareness, courage, psychological toughness, and a huge degree of specific conditioning. This conditioning requires players to develop a wide range of high-level fitness parameters, including strength, speed, power, agility, endurance, and coordination. In short, the modern player must be an athlete, and this term is used frequently in this book to emphasize this point. What is increasingly clear is that simply playing the game is not enough to develop the high level of specific fitness required to compete at the highest level. What is needed is a highly scientific program that effectively and efficiently prepares players to perform at this level.

The key to any soccer conditioning program is how well it transfers to enhanced soccer performance. It must be designed to ensure that basic scientific principles are adhered to. Similarly, it must be designed to maximize the transfer to soccer performance. This book is designed so that the scientific principles underlying conditioning programs are presented and that the specific requirements of soccer are explained and programs designed to address these needs. This emphasis on explaining the "why" as well as the "how" allows coaches and athletes to modify the programs to suit their specific needs, which is an important aspect of any training program.

Individual chapters are devoted to each of the key fitness variables required for top soccer performance. These chapters address the basic principles underlying each variable and provide key drills and exercises, thereby empowering the coach and athlete to construct individually based programs. These chapters are also broken down to allow for the sequential development of each variable, so that training can be geared to players at all levels of development.

Optimum progress in any training program is a balance between training and recovery. Unfortunately, recovery is too often ignored, resulting in less than optimal training progress. To this end, a chapter is presented that specifically addresses recovery and presents methods of optimizing recovery and regeneration, facilitating optimal gains in the program. Similarly, high-quality nutrition is an essential part of any training and recovery program and a chapter is devoted to this key area, again presenting a strategy that will facilitate optimum gains.

The book also provides the answers to three key questions: What do I do? When do I do it? How do I do it? It provides a complete year's training program that can be geared toward each individual's specific competition structure and level of development.

A key aspect of this book is that it has been planned in terms of the long-term development of the player, ensuring that they develop all of the key requirements of high-level performance. The developing player requires a system of long-term development that provides a road map to optimally develop their conditioning, ensuring that they reach more advanced levels of competition as complete players and with all the tools necessary to compete effectively. This book addresses this long-term process by identifying key phases within an athlete's development and providing specific exercises to be included in each phase, along with advice on constructing training sessions and programs for each phase. This book provides the soccer player with all the tools needed to maximize performance.

By following the system presented in this book, the soccer athlete is giving himself every chance to reach his full potential.

1

The Fitness Requirements of Soccer

When setting up an effective conditioning system for soccer, it is important to understand the exact requirements of the game. The quality of soccer performance depends upon a wide range of factors, such as skill level, teamwork, nutrition, and psychology, but a major feature of elite soccer performance is its dependence upon an advanced level of highly specific fitness. Modern soccer players are undoubtedly bigger, faster, and stronger than in the past, largely due to the introduction of scientifically based conditioning methods. However, soccer fitness is multifaceted and requires the development of a large number of fitness parameters, including strength, speed, power, agility, and endurance, all of which require a great deal of training to be optimally developed. To be optimally effective, the development program must be well-planned and incorporate all of the key fitness parameters. Conditioning methods are constantly evolving and players must ensure that they are utilizing the most modern, effective training methods, which must be incorporated into a long-term development plan.

An important starting point in constructing a soccer conditioning program is understanding the exact physical requirements of the game. The program also needs to take positional differences into consideration. Therefore, programs for different positions will need to be modified in terms of the exact physical requirements of each position.

Motion Analysis

In simple terms, soccer is an intermittent, high-intensity sport. The game lasts for 90 minutes (age-group games will differ), with the ball in play for a large proportion of this time. An important starting point in constructing an appropriate conditioning tool for soccer is to carefully analyze the exact movement patterns of the game. Motion analysis of soccer clearly shows the complexity of the movement patterns, with each game consisting of 1000 to1200 bouts of action, which can involve game-related activities (e.g., passing, tackling) or changes in pace and/or direction.

The work patterns involve changes of activity that occur every five or six seconds, with short rest pauses. Running patterns involve periods of walking (25 percent), jogging (37 percent), cruising submaximally (20 percent), sprinting (11 percent), and moving backward (7 percent), with each of these patterns involving multidirectional movements. Sprints average 16 yards (15 meters), and occur once every 30 seconds. In terms of time, the ratio of high-intensity to low-intensity movement is approximately 1:7.

Players normally cover between five and seven miles (eight and 12 kilometers) per match, although higher values have been recorded. However, this distance is covered in mostly five- to 11-yard (five- to 10-meter) runs. In addition, less than 2 percent of the total distance covered by players occurs with the ball, meaning that the vast majority of movement takes places without the ball. For much of the game, work intensities are high, with an average of 75 to 85 percent of maximum heart rate (MHR) reported. Available research suggests that heart rates are moderate (i.e., below 70 percent of MHR) for approximately 10 percent of the playing time, high (70 to 90 percent of MHR) for approximately 60 percent of the playing time, and very high (above 90 percent of MHR) for 30 percent of the playing time. This research shows the high-intensity nature of much of the game, and this pattern must be reflected in the training.

This high intensity is further emphasized by the fact that lactate is produced from the outset of the game. Increased blood lactate levels reflect the fact that anaerobic glycolytic processes contribute to energy production during soccer matches and thus need to be trained in addition to the ATP-PCr (phosphocreatine) and aerobic systems.

Movement Patterns

When looking at the key movements within a game, it becomes clear that the vast majority of soccer movements are multijoint and require high levels of coordinated strength and power in the major mobilizing muscles of the lower body. Large force capacity needs to be developed in this key power zone, and these forces also need to be developed rapidly, stressing the rate of force production. Triple extension at the hip, knee, and ankle is especially important, as it contributes to sprinting, accelerating, jumping, and changing directions. In addition, many movements require the transference of force from the lower-body power zone to the upper body and extremities. Therefore, force-transference movements must be trained. Because this force transference occurs through the torso region, core strength and stabilization must be stressed as well. A higher level of fat-free body weight is advantageous for some positions (e.g., central defender, striker) and for players whose game is being negatively affected by a lack of physical presence. In these situations, programs that stress muscle hypertrophy can be utilized.

Many key running movements occur at high speeds, with regular changes of speed and direction. This type of movement involves anaerobic endurance, especially in the ATP-PCr system, and the ability to tolerate lactic acid buildup. In addition, a high degree of speed and agility development is required. Speed needs to be stressed predominantly over short distances although some key positions (e.g., wingbacks) require excellent maximal speed over longer distances. Speed needs to be addressed as part of the training program in lateral, curvilinear, and linear directions. The ability to accelerate from both running starts and standing starts is essential for all positions. Agility development requires the ability to accelerate, decelerate, and perform multidirectional changes, all while maintaining good body position. Every player needs to develop the ability to either create space via multidirectional movements or to track players aiming to make this space. Therefore, the ability to read and react and to produce effective and efficient controlled movements in these situations must be developed, along with excellent balance and coordination skills.

Soccer presents a major challenge to the strength and conditioning professional. Optimally developing all of these parameters—with the ideal sequence of development—within both annual and long-term models requires a scientifically designed program. This book is designed to provide coaches and athletes with the tools to create scientifically sound training programs that conform to the requirements of long-term athlete development.

2

The Science of
Soccer Conditioning

To be optimally effective, training has to comply with basic sport science principles. The aim of any soccer conditioning program is to improve performance on the soccer field. Therefore, it is important to choose methods and programs that optimize the transfer from training to game performance. An understanding of the basic science that underpins training is an important element in constructing an effective training program. Programs that adhere to basic scientific principles are likely to both enhance performance and decrease the risk of injury. The programs described in this book are carefully planned to optimize the transfer of scientific information into effective training programs.

In general, coaches and athletes need to understand the basic science that underpins the physiology, mechanics, training principles, and motor-learning aspects of any conditioning program.

Basic Physiology of the Energy System

Prior to constructing an endurance program, the coach must have a fundamental knowledge of the basic physiological functions of the energy systems. All energy systems are concerned with regenerating ATP, the body's universal energy substrate. In fact, ATP is the only substance that the body can use to produce energy. However, the body's ATP stores are very small (approximately enough for one second of activity) and need to be constantly regenerated, either aerobically (i.e., with oxygen) or anaerobically (i.e., without oxygen). Anaerobic energy can be provided via two systems: the ATP-PCr system and the glycolytic system.

Anaerobic Physiology

The ATP-PCr system can sustain high-intensity exercise for six to 10 seconds. Phosphocreatine (PCr) is used to regenerate ATP, and this process continues until the PCr is depleted. Before this system can be used again, the PCr needs to be regenerated aerobically. This process is rapid, with 50 percent being regenerated within about 40 seconds and 100 percent within three minutes. The speed of this process allows an athlete to perform repeated high-intensity activities within a game. This energy system can be enhanced through appropriate training. Specific training for this system involves high-intensity exercise for approximately five seconds with 40 to 180 seconds of recovery.

The glycolytic system uses stored glycogen or blood glucose to regenerate ATP. This system can sustain high-intensity movement for up to 90 seconds, but the cost is the production of lactic acid, which quickly dissociates into lactate and H^+, thereby causing an increase in the acidity of the muscle and a resultant reduction in the quality of muscle contraction. The body must develop the enzymes needed to produce the energy as well the ability to release and neutralize large amounts of H^+. Training for the glycolytic system involves repeated high-intensity efforts of 20 to 90 seconds, interspersed with rest in a 1:3 to 1:5 ratio, depending upon the intensity of the effort, with greater effort requiring more rest.

The Aerobic System

ATP can also be regenerated aerobically, which has the potential to create a great deal of energy, far more than the other two systems. Despite this high capacity, it must be remembered that the aerobic system does not support high-intensity exercise. It therefore does not greatly contribute to some of the key high-intensity movements that dictate success in soccer. However, the aerobic system does play a key role in recovery between high-intensity bouts. Active recovery between exercise bouts (as occurs in a soccer game) provides a specific method of developing this system. Traditionally, an aerobic base, developed through extensive distance running, was recommended for all athletes. A more recent approach is that, unless aerobic performance is poor, this technique is not recommended, especially because it can negatively affect speed development by hindering neural speed pathways. Instead, utilize the methods presented in Chapter 10, which use the principles of interval training to provide a more soccer-specific method of enhancing aerobic performance.

If distance running is performed within a program, it needs to be of a low intensity, which targets the slow-twitch muscles, and should predominantly serve as a recovery session. Most work should focus on high-intensity movements aimed at enhancing maximum oxygen consumption (i.e., $\dot{V}O_2$max) and/or improving velocity at $\dot{V}O_2$max while minimizing the negative effects on speed and strength.

The Principles of Training

A key element in the application of sport science research has been the establishment of training principles. These principles have been consistently validated by scientific research and should form the basis of all training. Failing to maximally utilize them will certainly result in nonproductive training, and possibly result in a deterioration of performance and increased injury risk. The key training principles that have to be addressed within any training program are as follows:

- Specificity
- Overload
- Progression
- Fitness fatigue
- Rest and recuperation

- Individual differences
- Reversibility
- Periodization
- Long-term development

Specificity

To be effective, training must match—or be "specific" to—the exact requirements of the sport. Ongoing research has both confirmed the accuracy of this principle and shown that the degree of specificity is even greater than previously believed. Effective training is specific to the following:

- The energy systems used
- The speeds of movements used
- The muscles used
- The order of muscle recruitment
- The force requirements of the movement (in terms of direction, quantity, and speed)

The details outlined in Chapter 1 provide an excellent starting point for designing a soccer-specific conditioning program. All of the chapters in this book utilize methods that are highly specific to soccer, both physiologically and mechanically.

Overload

The body will only positively adapt to the stress of training if it is progressively subjected to increasing demands. Therefore, the program must be designed to place increasingly challenging demands on the body. In general, the quantity of stress placed on the body will depend upon two key program variables: intensity and volume. Intensity is the degree of stress imposed on the body from a dose of exercise. Volume is the total amount of training carried out.

In general, an inverse relationship exists between these two variables. As intensity increases, training volume must be reduced. It is important to decide if intensity or volume is the most appropriate method of providing overload, and then alter the training schedule accordingly.

Progression

Progression is the method by which overload is provided. Progression involves making appropriate incremental training demands and increasingly challenging the body to perform at a higher level. Progression can be created through changes in either volume or intensity. The preferred method will depend upon the parameter being trained and the phase of training. Sequencing appropriate progression is a challenging task, as too little progression will reduce overload and halt training progress. Too much progression, on the other hand, can cause overuse injuries or overtraining and again limit progress.

Fitness Fatigue

Fitness fatigue describes the body's response to a training dose (Figure 2-1). A training session has two major effects on the body: potentiation (i.e., an enhanced physical capacity) and a certain degree of fatigue. In the short term, the fatigue effect tends to

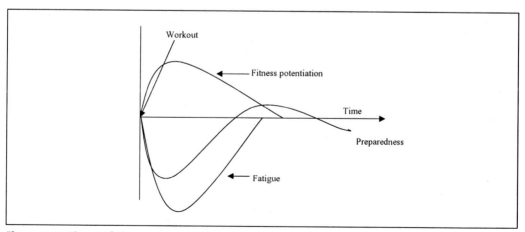

Figure 2-1. Fitness fatigue

be larger than the potentiation effect. Therefore, training preparedness, or the ability to perform, is temporarily lowered immediately following a workout. However, potentiation tends to last longer than fatigue, and so preparedness will increase after a certain amount of time. A key element of training is the balance between the two effects for optimal training results.

Rest and Recuperation

The body can only supercompensate and adapt to training stress when it is able to recover. Therefore, optimal development requires that the body recovers from the training stresses, while it is also important that sufficient training stresses are aimed at developing the required fitness parameters. Training must be sequenced to allow for appropriate recovery. Manipulations such as split routines and hard/easy days are also useful in ensuring adequate recovery. Excessive playing commitments will greatly affect a player's recovery ability and the quantity of quality training he can undertake. Periodized schedules are essential in allowing for the optimal development of an athlete's level of conditioning while allowing for optimal rest and recuperation. Full periodized schedules are outlined in Chapter 14. In addition, recovery methods such as whirlpools, cold baths, massage, and postexercise nutrition must be utilized in terms of enhancing recovery (refer to Chapter 13).

Individual Differences

Although the physiology of all athletes is the same, and every athlete's body will adapt in the same physiological way to training, the rate and quantity of adaptation will vary. One important factor is the individual tolerance to exercise. A training program that provides the ideal level of overload for one athlete may be insufficient for another and provide too great a stress for a third. While the first athlete would make good progress on the program, the second athlete would make little progress and the third would suffer from overtraining and make no progress. In addition to differences in training tolerance, some people are fast responders, meaning that they respond rapidly to a training stress. Others are slow responders who take a longer time before any significant changes are evident in response to the training program. Similarly, some people are high responders and make significant progress in relation to a program, while others are low responders who make little gain in response to a training dose. Obviously, a single training program will not optimally develop all players on a team. Ideally, each player will have an individualized program based upon his own specific requirements.

Reversibility

The "use it or lose it" maxim applies to all sports training. Any time training ceases or exercise intensity drops for a period of time, the associated conditioning level will drop as well. Some fitness parameters are lost more quickly than others. For example, aerobic fitness is lost more quickly than strength. This reduction in conditioning level in response to a drop in the intensity of work has important implications for the design of programs. In-season programs must maintain the levels of conditioning built during the preseason (e.g., strength and power work has to be performed during the season if performance is to be maintained). Off-season programs also must maintain any key fitness variables previously developed (e.g., to omit speed work at this time will be to the detriment of this key variable). In general, the volume of work needed to maintain a fitness variable is lower than that required to develop it. Therefore, lower-volume maintenance programs can be deployed to retain performance in one variable while emphasis is shifted to developing another.

Periodization

Periodization is the key to the optimal application of training stresses. It involves designing the training program around key phases of work and creating the optimal sequencing of training to arrive at the day of competition in peak fitness. Periodization involves splitting the year into a number of cycles, each with their own specific aim. The volume and intensity of various training methods are manipulated during these periods to optimally develop the athlete's conditioning throughout the year and to utilize the optimal sequencing of various fitness variables. A periodized program is outlined in Chapter 14.

Long-Term Development

The achievement of quality performance in late-maturation sports such as soccer involves setting up an effective program of development. Performance in many fitness variables is based upon sound conditioning basics (e.g., speed is dependent upon optimal technique). Therefore, players who have not developed this base are at a huge disadvantage compared to those who have. In addition, poor techniques developed at a younger age are very difficult to eradicate at a later date. It has also been shown that optimal ages exist for the development of fitness variables. For example, speed is best developed before the age of 16. Therefore, athletes who do not work on this variable at this time lose out on a huge development opportunity.

Peak performance at a young age does not necessarily relate to peak performance at more advanced levels. If the aim of a player is to perform at a higher level, then it is vital that the principles of long-term development are adhered to. Too many players aim to perform at a young age and omit the key work that will provide long-term development. Instead, they focus on methods that bring short-term results. This type of program precludes optimal performance at more advanced levels and is a reason why so many successful junior players do not make the transition to become successful older players.

The Training Model

The training model presented in this book consists of a pyramid with three phases—base, development, and peak—that provide sequential development (Figure 2-2). In many of the chapters, basic techniques must be mastered before more advanced workouts are attempted. This model provides for an optimal sequencing of training on each fitness parameter, facilitating ultimate high-level performance.

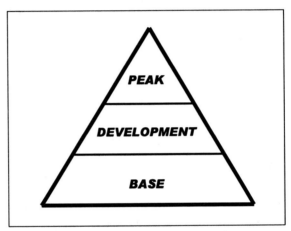

Figure 2-2. The training model

Base

At this level, the fundamental techniques and body conditioning associated with soccer-specific fitness parameters are developed (e.g., basic agility moves, speed techniques, and lifting techniques). Base-level training is often carried out in noncompetitive environments with the aim of honing technique so that it is maintained during the more advanced methods introduced in later stages. It is imperative for the optimal long-term progression that the base-level work is carried out and mastered prior to moving into the later stages. Even highly skilled players must master these skills if they wish to develop to their maximum potential.

The key aims of this phase are:

- To develop excellent movement mechanics for linear, lateral, and multilateral movement
- To build a high degree of balanced strength, stability, and mobility based on excellent core strength and control
- To develop basic resistance-training techniques
- To build a sound endurance base

Development

At this level, increasingly challenging tasks are introduced to the fundamental techniques developed in the base stage. Completing the base-conditioning period allows for more advanced methods to be introduced progressively at this new stage without overtaxing the body's recovery ability. Increasingly competitive methods are used, and the level of overload is progressively developed during this phase.

The key aims of this phase are:

- To hone the key movement mechanics of speed and agility in increasingly complex, high-speed, and competitive situations
- To develop a high level of functional body strength and control in key movements
- To develop muscle hypertrophy as appropriate
- To develop basic power-movement techniques
- To develop high levels of endurance
- To maintain the sound mobility base

Peak

This phase represents the expression of the potential developed in the prior two phases. Completion of the previous two phases ensures that techniques are maintained during the increasingly intense and position-specific drills introduced in the peak phase. Again, the body preparedness previously developed allows these more intense methods to be used without the risk of injury or stress overload that would be present otherwise.

The key aims of this phase are:

- To develop a high level of functional power
- To develop a high level of functional core strength and stability
- To develop a high level of speed and acceleration
- To develop a high level of random agility
- To reach peak endurance performance
- To maintain the sound mobility base

Within this pyramid development model, each fitness parameter has its own specific aims and objectives associated with each phase. In addition, athletes may be at different stages of each fitness parameter. For example, an athlete entering the system may have completed a regimen of strength training and is at the development stage of this parameter, but may have no experience with speed training and is therefore at the base level in this parameter. Regardless of soccer ability, each player must be assessed in his ability in each fitness parameter and then developed appropriately. Even top players often have not developed their basic techniques and skills in a number of areas, and their maximum performance is negatively affected. Their basic athleticism is sometimes lacking, so they never achieve their full potential. Therefore, these phases are essential to the player's future development and cannot be rushed. The player should only move on when the work in each phase has been totally mastered.

The long-term program should always take precedence over short-term aims. The current system of player development does not facilitate long-term development, as it features an overemphasis on matches, trials, and game preparations at a young age, as well as a lack of appropriate base development in the fitness parameters. Quality training and practice is far more important than playing at a young age, and playing commitments must not compromise the training program. In addition, training programs must be carefully planned. A shotgun approach to fitness simply cannot achieve optimum results and only a scientifically based long-term development program can help the player of the future achieve success.

The Principles of Skill Development

Many of the aspects of fitness that are required for soccer (e.g., speed, agility, and exercise technique) can be described as "skills." As such, they are subject to the general rules of skill acquisition. A general understanding of these rules can have a tremendous effect on the effectiveness of individual practice sessions and overall soccer programs.

The Amount of Quality Practice

The most important variable in skill development is undoubtedly the amount of quality practice. The basic exercises and techniques that will ultimately enhance soccer skills must be deliberately practiced if optimum performance is to be achieved. Even advanced athletes must continue to hone their basic techniques. This type of quality practice can be effectively incorporated into warm-up routines.

The Stages of Skill Development

When setting up appropriate training programs and sessions, it is important to ascertain the ability of the athlete in relation to the skill being developed. Three distinct phases of skill development have been identified.

The Verbal-Cognitive Stage

The aim of the athlete during this stage is to become acquainted with the task. As athletes at this stage are performing a movement, they are constantly thinking about the task and, as a result, movement tends to be relatively uncoordinated. The ability to focus on other aspects of performance is limited, as focus is simply on the task at hand. Although improvements are large and rapid, the motor programs for the task have not been well defined and refined, and mistakes are common. In general, the cognitive phase will coincide with the base phase, during which athletes are learning techniques.

The Motor Stage

At this stage, movement patterns have been defined, but still need to be refined. Again, perfect practice is vital to ensure the development of high-quality motor skills. Consistency and efficiency of movement will continue to improve through this phase, requiring increasingly challenging coaching interventions. Athletes will also be able to shift focus more effectively and often combine movements (e.g., dribbling a ball with the eyes focused on the playing environment). This stage is normally longer than the verbal stage and should be marked by appropriate progressions in the complexity of drills used. The motor stage generally coincides with the development phase.

The Autonomous Phase

This phase represents the highest end of the skill spectrum. In fact, some athletes never reach this phase. In the autonomous phase, actions are produced automatically with little or no attention placed on them. Motor programs are so efficient that they run with little or no attention, which means that they can run for longer durations and with greater efficiency. Athletes can react to games as they unfold. With this type of performer, it is vital that they experience challenging drills that develop these abilities. Performance improvements are slow at this point, as athletes are at the top end of the skill spectrum. This stage represents the high end of the peak phase.

Session Organization

When setting up a session, the coach has a number of key options that can impact the level of learning likely to come from the session. In terms of how to schedule drills within the session, two key questions must be addressed that directly influence skill development:

- How will time be allocated within the session?
- How will the drills and exercises be ordered within the session?

Massed Versus Distributed Practice

Massed practice generally refers to a situation in which little rest takes place between practice attempts or practice bouts. This type of practice allows for a great deal of work to be carried out in a given time period, but also can develop higher degrees of fatigue.

Distributed practice involves greater period of rest between practice attempts and practice bouts. This type of practice results in less work per unit of time, but allows fatigue to be dissipated more effectively.

The style used will depend upon the type of skill being developed and the players' stage of learning. Where fatigue buildup is detrimental to skill development (e.g., in a cyclic skill such as maximum speed development), a distributed practice system is more effective, whereas a massed practice may be more suitable for a discrete skill. Similarly, for athletes in the cognitive phase, where motor patterns are not well developed and where fatigue can be a major factor, a distributed session is recommended. Athletes in the late motor and autonomous phases are normally better equipped to handle massed practice, but even then the parameter being developed should dictate appropriate work/rest ratios. For example, maximum speed requires a distributed practice.

Blocked and Random Practice

When providing the optimal environment for skill development within a session, it is vital that the coach selects appropriate drills and activities and arranges them optimally within the session. Blocked and random allocations provide various methods by which activities and drills can be incorporated into a session.

In a blocked practice, tasks are grouped together so that the same task is repeated for the required number of sets and repetitions before the athlete moves on to the next task. In a random practice, a number of different tasks are performed in no particular order (e.g., switching among five different agility drills for each repetition in a circuit).

In general, blocked practice is effective for developing closed skills, such as strength-training movements. However, for open skills such as those found on the soccer field, available research suggests that while blocked practice results in the greatest short-term learning, random practice results in greater retention of skill and long-term performance enhancement. When a player is in the verbal-cognitive stage, blocked practice can be very useful. Random practice should start to dominate through the motor stage and dominate in the autonomous phase.

Drill Selection

While many excellent books and videos are available highlighting numerous drills and exercises that can be used to develop performance, the coach must use discretion in the utilization of these drills. During the planning of a session, it is important that the coach asks himself a number of key questions when selecting exercises:

- What do I want to achieve?
- What drills allow me to do this goal?

- What are the key aspects of the drill that I need to address to achieve my goals?

With the myriad of drills available, a coach can often get bogged down in coming up with new drills each week or simply showing his knowledge by introducing drill after drill. While this style of coaching can provide a variety of training, it is vital that the coach addresses the key elements of the game. A drill must be seen simply as a tool and not as an end in itself.

For example, a coach may need to develop the ability to produce a fast rate of foot turnover in a speed drill. He should then look at the options available to him and select appropriate drills. It is also vital that he notes the key points to address, such as landing on the balls of the feet, keeping the feet under the center of gravity, holding the arms at a 90-degree angle, moving the hands from "cheek to cheek," and keeping a good postural alignment.

Once the drills are placed within the session, the vital step is to coach, coach, coach. The coach must ensure that the athletes are picking up on the key elements highlighted and that they are being provided with the practice and feedback necessary to improve their performance.

The Speed/Accuracy Trade Off

In general terms, the faster a movement is performed, the lower the accuracy of the movement. Similarly, performing a movement too slowly can result in alterations of key movement patterns and hinder skill development. Therefore, an optimal speed exists for most skills, especially for speed and agility movements. An easy way in which the coach can establish this fact is to encourage the athletes to go as fast as they can before their technique breaks down. This rule should be applied to all of the agility and speed drills presented in this book. Clearly, this optimum speed will vary between individuals, but by carefully planning sessions, coaches can allow all athletes to work at their optimum level.

Guidelines for Optimizing Skill Development

The development pyramid for many of the fitness variables is set up so that the three phases (base, development, and peak) correspond generally with the three stages of skill development. The following guidelines are given for athletes at each of the three phases.

Guidelines for Coaching Athletes in the Base Phase

- Focus on a single task or skill.
- Use quality instructions, demonstrations, and other cues to facilitate learning.

- Carry each skill out in a noncompetitive environment until the movement pattern is well developed.
- Break down skills into smaller parts when appropriate.
- Develop the skill correctly via a high quality of practice.
- Do not allow fatigue to interfere with the skill-learning process.
- Choose a small number of exercises and drills.
- Use distributed practices to minimize the effect of fatigue on skill development.
- Use blocked practices to develop basic skill patterns.

Guidelines for Coaching Athletes in the Development Phase

- Gradually shift from closed to open drills.
- Gradually shift from simple to complex patterns.
- Gradually increase the competition on each drill (e.g., speed competitions).
- Progressively increase the variety of drills and exercises.
- Reduce the quantity of feedback, while increasing its precision.
- Increasingly encourage the athletes to analyze their own performance by using appropriate questions.
- Start to vary training sessions with more frequency as the athletes move through this phase (including strength training).
- Use increasingly varied and random practice distributions on open skills (e.g. agility).

Guidelines for Coaching Athletes in the Peak Phase

- Use a variety of complex drills that involve read-and-react situations.
- Use a great number of random skills.
- Vary session regularly (including strength training).
- Provide very precise but less frequent feedback.
- Develop the athletes' ability to use external and internal feedback mechanisms to answer performance-related questions and reduce the dependency on the coach.
- Allow random practice distribution to dominate on agility drills.

3

Assessing Performance

Any strength and conditioning program aims to develop athletes who have improved levels of fitness that can transfer into improved soccer performance. Therefore, a key element of establishing success is monitoring performance and progress. To facilitate this process, valid and reliable measures of fitness performance are needed to accurately assess the level of performance, identify areas of strength and weakness, and assess progress within the program. While soccer performance is subjectively assessed, fitness parameters can be objectively measured via a carefully selected battery of tests designed to assess all of the major fitness parameters that affect soccer performance. It is important to note that the applicability each test has to performance will, to a large extent, depend upon the player's position, which must be taken into consideration when interpreting the test results.

The Tenets of Quality Testing

For testing to have any value, it is imperative that it is closely controlled and produces accurate results. It is important to ensure that any possible sources of measurement error are minimized, and that changes in performance can be attributed to the player's fitness improvements and not to other factors. Three key areas of focus in testing are validity, reliability, and objectivity.

Validity

Validity refers to the degree to which a test actually measures the variable it purports to measure. The tests outlined in this section are selected to test specific aspects of soccer performance. Using such a battery of tests enables the coach to measure and analyze the key fitness variables.

Reliability

Reliability refers to the reproducibility of scores. Ideally, no variation should exist in scores between tests carried out within a short period of time. To maximize reliability, the coach should ensure the following:

- The testing conditions are identical for each testing period (e.g., surface, indoors/outdoors, measuring instruments).
- Athletes must use identical equipment, footwear, etc.
- Tests always follow the same testing order.
- Testing is done at the same time, with the same pretesting protocols (e.g., timing of meals, pretest warm-ups).
- Testing uses identical equipment and utilizes standard testing protocols.
- Standardized recording systems are used.
- Athletes are rested, with at least one day of rest before the testing session.

Objectivity

Objectivity refers to the degree of conformity between scores produced by different testers. Ideally, the same tester should administer all tests. However, this consistency is not always possible. It is therefore essential that all testers are well trained and follow standard protocols.

Tests to Evaluate Soccer Conditioning

No one test can give the coach all the information needed to evaluate a player's performance. Therefore, a battery of tests must be used. The battery in Figure 3-1 is designed to evaluate all aspects of soccer performance.

If the tests are to be carried out in a single day, the order outlined in Figure 3-1 provides for a suitable schedule. In general, all short-duration tests that result in little fatigue should be carried out early in the day and the longer-duration, high-fatigue tests should be carried out later in the day. The tests may also be split into different days, provided that they comply with the reliability guidelines.

Fitness Parameter	Subdivision	Test
Anthropometry		Height Weight Body fat (skinfolds)
Speed	Pure acceleration Transition acceleration Maximum speed	10-yard dash 40-yard dash Flying 40-yard dash
Agility		T-test Pro agility
Power	Functional leg strength Explosive strength/power	Vertical jump 1 RM rack/hang clean
Strength	Leg strength Upper-body strength	1 RM squat 1 RM bench press
Endurance	Anaerobic endurance Aerobic endurance	Repeated sprint test Multistage test
Note: 1 RM = one-repetition maximum		

Figure 3-1. A battery of soccer tests

Anthropometry

Height and weight are the basic measurements of an athlete's anthropometry. However, for optimal application these values must be supplemented by a measure of the athlete's body-fat levels. High levels of body fat compromise athletic performance and therefore should be minimized. Any weight-gain programs must emphasize the development of lean muscle mass. Body-fat scores give an excellent indication of the relative distribution of weight or weight gain in terms of lean mass and fat mass.

A cost-effective method of assessing body composition involves the use of skinfolds. A number of options are available, including the measurement of the following seven locations:

- Chest
- Midaxillary
- Triceps
- Subscapular
- Abdomen
- Anterior suprailiac
- Thigh

To ensure the validity and reliability of measurements, skinfolds should always be taken by highly trained personnel. Players should try to have a body-fat percentage of less than 12 percent, preferably in the range of 7 to 10 percent.

Speed Dashes

Soccer involves runs over a range of distances. The speed test battery involves speed testing over the following distances:

- 10 yards
- 40 yards
- Flying 40 yards

The three elements of this test assess the three key aspects of speed performance: the 10-yard test allows for the assessment of pure acceleration, the 40-yard dash assesses transition acceleration, and the flying 40-yard dash assesses maximum speed. All of these tests require electronic timing for reliability. A hand-held stopwatch will give unreliable results that cannot be used for assessment. The runs should be carried out on a surface that remains constant at all times of the year, such as a running track or turf field.

The 10- and 40-Yard Dashes

Infrared beams should be set up at the 10- and 40-yard lines, with a start switch at the start (Figure 3-2). The athlete should start from his preferred stance behind the starting line, with his hand on the start switch. He then self-starts and sprints through the beams as quickly as possible. Times will be taken for both the 10-yard and 40-yard dash in the same run.

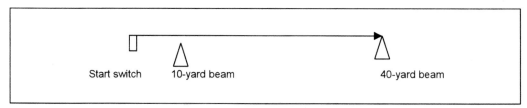

Figure 3-2. 10- and 40-yard dashes

Flying 40-Yard Dash

For the flying 40-yard dash test, two beams are set up and the player is given an acceleration zone of up to 30 yards (Figure 3-3). The athlete sprints through the acceleration zone so that he is at top speed when he reaches the first beam. He then sprints through to the second beam, where the time is taken and recorded. On all tests, three trials are allowed, and the best performance is recorded.

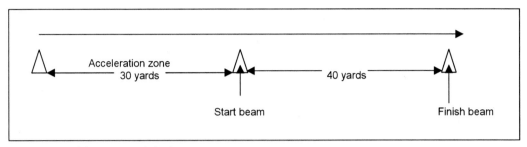

Figure 3-3. Flying 40-yard dash

Agility

Agility is an important aspect of superior soccer performance, and the testing battery utilizes the T test and the pro agility test to give an indication of a player's ability in this area. The T test involves forward running, side-shuffling, and backpedaling, while the pro agility test assesses acceleration, deceleration, and changes of direction off both the right and left legs.

T Test

A course is set up in the shape of a T, as shown in Figure 3-4, with an electronic beam at cone A. The players:

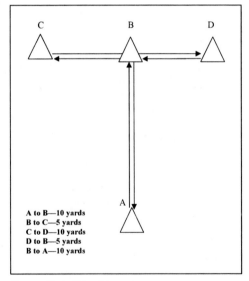

Figure 3-4. T test

- Self-start through the beam, sprint from cone A to cone B, and touch the base of cone B with the right hand.

- Side shuffle left to cone C, touching its base with the left hand.

- Side shuffle right to cone D, touching its base with the right hand.

- Shuffle left to cone B, touching its base with the left hand.

- Backpedal past cone A to stop the clock.

Coaching Points:

- Always have the players touch the base of each cone.

- On the side shuffle, the players must face front and not cross their feet.

Pro Agility Test

The coach sets up the course in the layout shown in Figure 3-5, with an electronic beam at cone A. The players stand at cone A, looking straight ahead and toward the coach. The players:

- Self-start and sprint from cone A to cone B and touch the base of cone B.
- Sprint from cone B to cone C, touching the base of the cone.
- Sprint past cone A, breaking the beam.

Coaching Points:

- Always have the players touch the base of each cone.
- Electronic timing should be utilized.

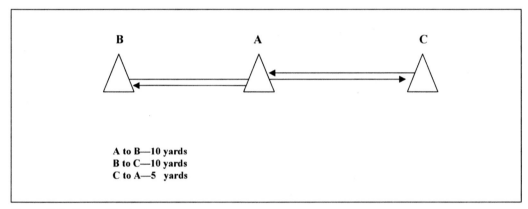

B **A** **C**

A to B—10 yards
B to C—10 yards
C to A—5 yards

Figure 3-5. Pro agility test

Strength Tests

Body strength is an important aspect of performance. Strength testing should not be introduced until the technique of each specific exercise is mastered. The following exercises are utilized as strength tests:

- Squat
- Bench press
- Rack/hang clean (for athletes in the peak phase)

After an appropriate warm-up, select a weight that the athlete thinks he can lift in good form using an Olympic bar (for a description of exercises, see Chapter 7). If the player is successful, then the weight is raised in an appropriate progression until the athlete fails. Attempt to ensure that the player reaches his maximum within five lifts.

Squat

The squat gives an excellent indication of all-round leg strength (Figure 3-6). The test uses a parallel squat, meaning that the player should lower the weight until his thighs are parallel to the floor.

Bench Press

The bench press gives a good indication of all-round upper-body strength (Figure 3-7).

Figure 3-6

Figure 3-7

Rack/Hang Clean

This exercise can be used to test explosive strength in the peak phase, which is vital for optimal soccer performance (Figure 3-8).

Figure 3-8

Vertical Jump

This exercise tests the player's ability to exert forces rapidly and can be seen as an indication of functional leg strength. The player rubs chalk on the fingers of his dominant hand. He then stands with the dominant shoulder approximately six inches from a wall, reaches up as high as possible with his feet flat on the floor, and makes a mark on the wall. He then jumps as high as possible from a two-foot takeoff, marking the wall at the highest point of the jump. Three jumps are performed and the highest jump is taken. Record the difference between the initial mark and the highest point. Increasingly, more sophisticated equipment, such as jump mats, are available to measure vertical jump performance. If available these tools should be utilized.

Anaerobic Endurance

The key actions in soccer are intense and are fueled by the anaerobic energy system, which acts in the absence of oxygen. The anaerobic system has two components: the ATP-PCr system and the anaerobic glycolytic system. Soccer sprints tend to be in short bursts, and so the ATP-PCr system is the most important. This system can be assessed via repeated sprint performance and the fatigue ratio (i.e., the difference between the athlete's best score and his worse score). It is important that the athlete exerts maximal efforts in each run. The best score is also recorded as a baseline figure for reference.

Repeated Sprint Test

The athlete completes six 40-yard dashes, with 30 seconds of recovery between each. Times are recorded for each run and the fatigue ratio is calculated by taking the difference between the fastest and slowest times, dividing that figure by the fastest time, and multiplying the figure by 100.

Fatigue ratio = (slowest score − peak score)/peak score x 100

Aerobic Endurance

Testing aerobic endurance requires utilization of the multistage fitness test, a commercially available test (www.1st4sport.com) that provides an indirect predictive test for $\dot{V}O_2$max. Two lines of cones are set up 20 meters apart. Using the multistage fitness test CD, the player runs between each set of cones to the timing set by a series of beeps. This practice is continued until the player cannot keep up with the beeps. The level and shuttle number at which the athlete pulls out is recorded and converted into a $\dot{V}O_2$max score.

Annual Testing Schedule

The number of testing periods will depend largely on the coach's preference and the team's playing program. However, it is important that sufficient testing periods are included to allow the coach to evaluate the players' strengths and weaknesses and to guide the design of the strength and conditioning program. Ideally, tests should be carried out at the following times.

- Prior to the start of the off-season period, allowing for the identification of strengths and weaknesses that can be worked on during the off-season period
- Prior to the precompetition period, to evaluate the success of the off-season workouts
- Immediately prior to the start of competition, to evaluate the success of the entire preparatory period and to assess the condition of players entering competition
- At midseason, to evaluate how the players are maintaining their condition through the season and identify any key needs

4

Workout Preparation

All training sessions should be preceded by a warm up-period, which must be viewed as "workout preparation" and a fundamental part of the program. A proper warm-up enhances the quality of the subsequent work, while also reducing the risk of injury. The workout preparation should involve three main areas of focus:

- Raising of body temperature
- Dynamic mobilization
- Innervation

Time is a precious commodity when training athletes, and so maximum use must be made of all training time. Therefore, workout preparation should always work on mechanics and mobilization development. This focus increases the time allocated each week to these areas and also increases the time the athlete has to master movements. In addition, a focused workout preparation period prepares the athlete to go immediately into the rest of the session.

Raising Body Temperature

The emphasis during a warm-up should be on quality movements and quality mechanics. Workout preparation can commence with basic movements occurring between two cones set 10 yards apart. The movement patterns outlined in this section can be effectively incorporated into the workout preparation, and also facilitate the development of good movement mechanics. For more details on these movements, refer to Chapter 6.

These movements should be performed at an increasing tempo, starting slowly but getting faster through the period—although they never reach high intensities. Upon completion, all athletes will have raised their body temperatures significantly, but also will have carried out a number of key drills to develop mechanics.

Forward/Backpedal (Figure 4-1 and 4-2)—The athlete runs forward 10 yards and then backpedals back to the starting line, repeating this pattern four times.

Figure 4-1   Figure 4-2

Side Shuffle (Figure 4-3)—Using a side-shuffle movement, the athlete moves between the two cones four times.

Figure 4-3

Carioca (Figure 4-4)—The athlete moves between the two cones using a carioca step pattern, repeating this action three times.

High Knee Walk (Figure 4-5)—The athlete uses a high knee walk to move from cone to cone three times, increasing the range and speed of motion from a walk to a skip on each repetition.

Figure 4-4

Figure 4-5

Dynamic Mobilization

A number of exercises can be introduced to mobilize the key muscles to be utilized in the forthcoming session. Most of these exercises can be performed with athletes moving between two cones set 10 yards apart, as in the previous sequence.

Lunges

Lunges provide a highly effective method of mobilizing a large number of muscles through dynamic movement. Emphasis should be on keeping the front knee at a 90-degree angle with the ground, with proper knee and ankle alignment. The body should be kept upright and firm. The back leg should come down to a point just above the ground. Arm action should mimic the sprinting action (Figure 4-6). Once the basic lunge has been mastered other progressions include the following advanced movements.

Figure 4-6

Overhead Lunge (Figure 4-7)—In the overhead lunge, both arms are raised overhead and the hands push way to emphasize spinal elongation.

Lunge With Twist (Figure 4-8)—In this exercise, the body is twisted toward the front knee, thereby providing a stretch in the transverse plane.

Lunge With Diagonal Rotation (Figure 4-9)—The body is rotated diagonally toward the front knee, bringing the left hand to the right foot and vice versa. This movement provides upper-body mobilization in the frontal plane, in addition to the movement provided by the lunge itself.

Figure 4-7

Figure 4-8

Figure 4-9

Backward Lunge (Figure 4-10)—The backward lunge provides an additional mobilization stimulus through the performance of large backward steps.

Lunge With Upper-Body Rotation (Figure 4-11)—This exercise is an excellent all-around moblizer. The athlete lunges forward with the right leg and then brings the left elbow to touch the right ankle.

Figure 4-10   Figure 4-11

Squat

The squat provides a multijoint stretch that also can be used to assess functional-movement capacity. The athlete assumes a position with the feet facing front and positioned approximately shoulder-width apart. He unlocks the hips and knees and assumes a full squat position, aiming to get the glutes as close to the floor as possible while maintaining a straight back. The heels should remain in contact with the floor and the feet should not rotate outward (Figure 4-12). He holds the position for about one-half second and then returns to the starting position. He completes a set of eight repetitions. Progression of the squat movement includes raising first one arm and then two arms while attempting to maintain the upright position.

Figure 4-12

Calf Walk With Shoulder Rotation (Figure 4-13)

This exercise provides mobility around both the ankle and shoulder joints. The athlete walks high onto the balls of the feet while simultaneously circling both arm as close to the ears as possible. He should hold the high position for about one second, and then continue. The one-second hold will give a good assessment of ankle integrity, as a tendency to roll out can indicate a weakness at this joint.

Hip Circles (Figures 4-14 and 4-15)

The hip joint is fundamental to most movements and therefore must be mobile. In this exercise, the athlete circles the hip in wide circles in both directions. He must repeat the movement for 10 total repetitions.

Figure 4-13

Figure 4-14

Figure 4-15

Walking-Forward Hip Circles (Figure 4-16)

Walking-forward hip circles further develop hip mobilization. While moving between the cones, the athlete abducts the right knee to 90 degrees. From this position, he rotates the knee forward until it faces straight ahead with 90 degrees of hip flexion.

Walking Backward Hip Circles (Figure 4-17)

To perform this exercise, the athlete flexes the hip to 90 degrees and then rotates the leg backward until it reaches the side of the body. He must alternate legs for the given distance.

Figure 4-16   Figure 4-17

Standing Stiff-Leg Dead Lifts (Figures 4-18 and 4-19)

The athlete stands upright with both hands overhead. He simultaneously extends the right leg backward and bends forward to touch the toes of the left foot. He performs the required number of repetitions and then repeats the movement with the other leg.

Figure 4-18   Figure 4-19

Inchworm (Figure 4-20 and 4-21)

The athlete assumes a press-up position. Keeping the legs practically straight, he slowly inches the feet forward until further stretch is impossible. He then reaches forward and repeats the movement for the given distance.

Figure 4-20   Figure 4-21

Stretch, Bend, and Go (Figures 4-22 through 4-24)

This exercise is an excellent total-body mobilizer. The athlete stands upright with his arms extended overhead and fingers interlocked. He pushes the fingers away from the body so that he feels a stretch through the upper body, and then bends to the side as far as possible without flexing or extending in the spine. At the point of maximum stretch, he flexes the spine and brushes the toes with the hands in a circular motion before returning to the start position. He then repeats the movement on the opposite side until he completes the required number of repetitions.

Figure 4-22   Figure 4-23   Figure 4-24

Innervations

This portion of the workout preparation is normally used in running-based sessions. It includes the performance of faster movements, either linear or lateral, to stimulate the neural pathways. The exact drills used will depend upon whether a lateral or linear emphasis is needed. Ladders can be utilized, as they are useful tools for developing movement patterns with large numbers of athletes in a small area. Although ladders are utilized for innervation, it is important to limit their use, as athletes have a tendency to look down at their feet during ladder drills, which is not recommended for optimal sprint and agility technique. During ladder and innervation drills, mechanics must be stressed with emphasis on the full PAL (posture, arm action, and leg action) system.

Linear Innervation

Linear innervation can be achieved equally through the use of speed ladders or by utilizing sprint drills that emphasize rapid foot turnover.

One Step per Hole (Figures 4-25 and 4-26)—This exercise is essentially a fast-feet drill in which each foot is placed in each successive ladder hole.

Figure 4-25   Figure 4-26

Two Steps per Hole (Figures 4-27 through 4-29)—In this exercise, the speed of movement is increased, as two steps are taken per hole (i.e., left in, right in, left forward).

In and Out—The athletes go through the ladder in a one-step manner (as shown in Figures 4-25 and 4-26) and then accelerate out of the ladder for five yards. Emphasis should be on fast, short strides as the athlete sprints out, which brings the focus to rapid leg action during acceleration.

Figure 4-27

Figure 4-28

Figure 4-29

Lateral Innervation

Side Shuffle (Figures 4-30 through 4-32)—The athlete side shuffles through the ladder with his feet being placed in each hole. Ensure that the athlete moves both ways through the ladder.

Figure 4-30

Figure 4-31

Figure 4-32

The Ickey Shuffle (Figures 4-33 through 4-36)—Named after former NFL player Ickey Woods, this movement develops the ability to move laterally through a small space. Starting at the side of the ladder, the athlete places one leg in the first hole and then the second foot in that same hole. The first foot then moves to the far side of the ladder and the second is placed forward into the next hole and the pattern continues (Figures 4-33 through 4-36).

Figure 4-33

Figure 4-34

Figure 4-35

Figure 4-36

5

Speed Training

Speed is regarded by many soccer coaches to be one of the most important aspects of soccer performance, which explains the emphasis placed on it in many testing and selection policies. Speed was once thought of as a genetically determined factor, but it is now generally acknowledged that speed can be improved with a scientifically designed program of training. It must be noted that the 100-meter-sprint model does not necessarily provide an ideal model upon which to base a soccer-specific speed program. Distances in soccer tend to be shorter and movement tends to be multilateral. Therefore, it is important to break down the specific speed and agility requirements of the specific position prior to constructing speed and agility programs.

Speed and agility training must not occur in isolation. Effective speed and agility performance is based upon appropriate conditioning in a number of areas. Essentially, speed and agility are dependent on explosive force. Therefore, all training methods that impact this aspect of performance need to be addressed. A "speed" athlete needs appropriate strength and power development (in terms of impulse production and reactive ability), appropriate flexibility, low levels of body fat, and the speed endurance to be able to sustain the quality of performance over the duration of the game.

Aspects of Speed

Running speed is directly linked to the relationship between stride length and stride cadence. Of the two, stride length is easier to improve and is related to the ground-reaction forces developed during running. Speed, therefore, is directly related to the speed-strength characteristics of the leg and hip musculature, and strength and power training is a vital part of any speed-development program. Stride cadence, which is the speed of each stride taken, is generally considered to be more difficult to improve. However, it can be improved through the efficacious use of sprint drills and sprint-assisted methods.

In most sports, including soccer, the key factor is often the ability to accelerate, rather than peak speed. Acceleration refers to the rate of change of velocity over time. Distances run in soccer are often short, and players need to be able to reach optimal velocity as quickly as possible. Soccer requires the ability to move from stationary positions and from rolling-type starts, and both scenarios need to be addressed within the program. Soccer also requires acceleration in multiple directions, and these need to be practiced (see Chapter 6 for turning techniques).

Running Mechanics

Effective speed requires effective technique. Mechanically sound running mechanics allow for effective force transmission and efficient timing of actions, thereby allowing for optimal stride length and stride cadence. In general, two mechanical models can be identified.

- Acceleration model
- Maximum-speed model

For both models, coaching emphasis should be on three areas:

- Body alignment
- Arm action
- Leg action

The Acceleration Model (Figure 5-1)

The acceleration model is shown in Figure 5-1, and three key features can be identified.

Figure 5-1

Body Alignment

During this phase, a pronounced forward lean of the body takes place, with a straight line generated from head to toe. It is important that this lean is a whole-body lean that does not come via a bending forward at the hips.

Arm Action

Arm action must always occur at the shoulder. In the acceleration model, the arm action is powerful and involves a greater range of motion than in the maximum-speed model. The feeling should be of driving the arm backward onto the hip. Hand position is to an extent a matter of preference, with either an open hand or loosely cupped action being suitable, but at no time should the hands be clenched or any tension be developed.

Leg Action

Ground contact time is at its greatest during acceleration, which allows for greater ground forces to be applied. A powerful push back into the ground should be developed via triple extension at the hip, knee, and ankle during the drive phase. Foot contact is always on the ball of the foot. This drive is then followed by a powerful drive of the knee forward and upward. After this motion, the knee angle closes and the leg goes into recovery. Then, the shin is thrust out and down into the following support-and-drive phase. During the initial strides, foot contact will occur in front of the center of gravity, with this distance decreasing as speed increases.

The Maximum Speed Model
(Figure 5-2)

The maximum speed model is shown in Figure 5-2, and again three key features can be identified.

Body Alignment

At maximum speed, the feeling should be of running tall, as if being pulled up by a balloon attached to the head. The hips should not be allowed to sink, as this negatively affects stride length. The head should be kept in alignment with the body, and the eyes should look straight ahead.

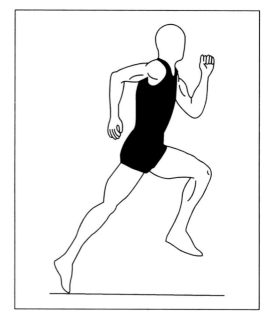

Figure 5-2

Arm Action

Arm action needs to occur at the shoulder and must be powerful but relaxed, emphasizing driving the arm backward to the hip. The arm angle should be held at approximately 90 degrees throughout, although some extension behind and flexion to the front does occur. The hand should come back just past the hips and brush close to the hips as it moves. In front, the hand will come up to approximately chin level. The hands should be held in the preferred position, with no tension present.

Leg Action

Leg action involves a powerful driving of the knee forward and upward, with a simultaneous closing of the knee angle, which reduces the lever arm. This action allows for the knee to be brought forward faster and is vital for an optimum stride cadence. Following the knee drive, the lower leg extends during late recovery and makes contact with the ground with a clawing striking action. The feeling should be of pulling the ground backward behind the body. Foot contact should be approximately under the center of gravity to avoid any braking effect and should occur on the balls of the feet. The leg should then actively push into the ground to provide the necessary ground-reaction forces for effective stride-length development, with a triple extension at the hip, knee, and ankle.

Soccer-Specific Speed

Soccer requires the ability to run at optimal speed many times during a game. This ability is often a crucial factor in both offensive and defensive success. In setting up the soccer speed program it is vital to examine the exact requirements of each playing position. Factors to consider include the following:

- The distance sprinted—This factor will determine how much training needs to be devoted to accelerative and maximal speed work. For soccer, most sprints need to be carried out over relatively short distances. However, wingers, wingbacks, fullbacks, and certain midfield players need to include longer-distance sprints to reflect the requirements of the game.

- The directional requirements—In soccer, multidirectional movement is common and the speed program needs to take this fact into account by incorporating soccer-specific multidirectional runs. The speed and agility sections must not be performed in isolation and need to be optimally combined in terms of drills and practice.

- The initial velocity—Some positions require an athlete to start from a stationary position, whereas others require an acceleration of an athlete already in motion. Again, training needs to take these factors into account. Wingers, for example, should work on their ability to accelerate from a running start as well as from a standing start.

- Recovery times—When recovery times are incomplete, speed endurance becomes an important aspect that needs to be trained separately.

The Long-Term Development of Speed

When developing speed, it is important to work on a long-term plan. It is vital that young athletes are introduced to speed training early, as the window of opportunity for speed development opens and closes at a young age. After this period, speed improvements occur mainly through enhanced power output. In the early stages, it is vital to develop basic sprint mechanics and a sound strength base. Only when these foundations are present can the other methods, such as sprint loading and sprint-assisted training, be effectively applied. The following pattern of progression is recommended.

Base Program

Initial speed-development work needs to focus on technique development. This training needs to be done initially in uncompetitive situations. The majority of the work is carried out with a goal of developing running technique and increasing the ability to run at optimal speed with good technique.

Development Program

Once the basic speed techniques have been developed, athletes can move into the development phase. At this point, the impetus is to maintain the technique developed in increasingly competitive situations (e.g., introducing runs against partners or ball-drop drills). In addition, increased loading is added to the techniques via the use of resisted runs, which develop sport-specific strength.

Peak Program

The peak program can be utilized when working with advanced athletes. At this stage, extremely high-quality and competitive work is carried out. Sprint-assisted programs are added and resisted programs are included as appropriate. Technique work is still performed to hone running technique. At all times during any speed session, the focus should be on quality, maximal work, with rest periods adequate to ensure that each effort is a maximal effort.

The Practice of Speed Development

Soccer speed-development programs will vary, but they normally include the following components:

- Technical development
- Running at optimal speed (The term "optimal speed" is used to emphasize the importance of technique. Although the aim is to run as fast as possible, excellent technique should always be used.)

- Sprint loading
- Sprint-assisted training
- Speed endurance

Technical Development

In any soccer speed program, it is vital that the athlete is trained to move as efficiently and effectively as possible. It is also essential that an effective sprinting technique be stressed from day one. Technique drills provide effective tools with which to develop effective techniques. It is important that the coach identifies the key technique elements to be developed and then selects and utilizes appropriate technique drills. The following drills provide options that help develop each of the key areas of technique (i.e., arm action, body alignment, and leg action).

Arm Action Drill

Arm Swings (Figures 5-3 and 5-4)

Objective: To develop a relaxed and powerful arm action

Description: In a standing position, imagine that you are holding a glass of liquid in each hand. Practice your arm action as if bringing the glass to your mouth on the upswing and ensuring that nothing is tipped on the way back. Increasingly beat down on the back swing and emphasize the drive during this motion.

Figure 5-3   Figure 5-4

Coaching Points:

- Arm action should occur at the shoulder joint.

- The shoulders are held low and relaxed.

- The arms swing straight forward, almost brushing the clothing.

- The hands are relaxed (either open or cupped, but not clenched).

- A 90-degree angle is maintained at the elbows.

Variations:

- This drill can be performed while seated.

- The drill can be developed into a more powerful action by emphasizing powerfully driving the arms backward.

- Resistance can be added in the form of bands.

Acceleration Posture Drills

A key in this area is to encourage the athletes to develop an effective forward lean. This position assists in the driving forward from an effective low position, which is essential for effective acceleration.

Partner Fall (Figure 5-5)

Objective: To develop a feel for the forward-lean acceleration position

Description: With a partner positioned approximately two to three feet in front of you, slowly fall forward to a point where your body forms an approximate 45-degree angle with the ground.

Coaching Points:

- Ensure a straight body position.

- Ensure that the athletes do not bend at the hips.

- The head should be held in a neutral position and be in line with the body.

Figure 5-5

Fall Forward and Sprint (Figure 5-6)

Objective: To develop the idea of maintaining a low body position when accelerating and of getting the foot down rapidly to enable optimum acceleration

Description: From a standing position, fall forward and then sprint off for five to 10 yards. The key to this drill is to emphasize the forward-body-lean element of acceleration and to get the foot down rapidly after the fall.

Figure 5-6

Coaching Points:

- Have the athletes focus on performing a full drive from the back leg.
- No flexion should occur at the hip during the fall.
- The foot should be placed down rapidly.
- The knee drive should be powerful.
- Have the athletes focus on a rapid first few strides.
- Arm action must be rapid and powerful.
- The athletes must alternate using the right and left foot first.

Stride and Lift Action Drills

These drills aim to develop some key areas of effective running mechanics: knee lift, front-leg reach and active recovery; back-leg push, and effective ankle action. These drills can be performed at different speeds and in different combinations, which assists in randomizing the drill set-up. The speed and method of each drill should reflect the athlete's ability. In general, drills can progress from standing, marching, and skipping, to full speed, and can also use repetitions on alternate legs or on the same leg. The focus should always be on form, and any change of speed should not cause a change in the performance.

Knee Lift (Figure 5-7)

Objective: To encourage a powerful knee drive

Description: Knee-lift drills involve an exaggerated raising of the knees, with the aim of having the upper thigh rise to a position parallel to the floor. This drill can be performed in place, marching, skipping, or at full speed.

Figure 5-7

Coaching Points:

- Athletes should always land on the balls of the feet.
- Athletes should push down with the supporting leg as the knee comes up, aiming to drive the supporting leg into triple extension.

- Athletes must dorsiflex the foot as it lifts off of the ground.

- Light, rapid foot contact should be used.

- The body should be upright or tilted slightly forward. It must not lean backward.

- The athlete should "walk tall."

- Each athlete should use a speed suitable to his ability, and then progress to full speed as appropriate.

- Effective and coordinated arm action must be used at all times.

Note: In addition, tools such as mini-hurdles can be utilized to develop the knee lift.

Down and Ups (Figure 5-8)

Objective: To encourage a light, fast ground contact

Description: This drill is a modification of the Knee Lift in which you bring the foot down and back up in a skipping-like action. The emphasis should be on attaining a low ground-contact time, with the ground effort bouncing the foot up into the high-knee position. This drill can be performed in place, marching, skipping, or at full speed.

Figure 5-8

Coaching Points:

- Athletes should always land on the balls of the feet.

- Remind the athletes to push down with the supporting leg as the knee comes up, achieving triple extension in the supporting leg.

- Athletes must dorsiflex the foot as it lifts off of the ground.
- Encourage light, rapid foot contact and the feeling of running tall.
- Effective and coordinated arm action must be used at all times.

Butt Kickers (Figure 5-9)

Objective: To develop an active leg recovery cycle by achieving a very low angle between the shin and thigh

Description: This action is coordinated with an effective knee lift. As the knee lifts, the lower leg swings back to contact the buttocks, resulting in a shortening of the lever arm. It is important to bring the heel simultaneously forward and up, and to coordinate this movement with a powerful knee lift, as this action is what actually occurs during sprinting. This drill can be performed in place, marching, skipping, or at full speed.

Figure 5-9

Coaching Points:

- The knee lift is performed first.
- The knees are not kept low during the movement, but instead drive up and forward as in a natural sprinting action.
- The forward and upward motion results in a rapid butt-kicking action.
- The feet should not extend beyond the body to the rear.
- Ground contact should be under the center of gravity and on the balls of the feet.
- Emphasize effective and coordinated arm action.

Cycling (Figure 5-10)

Objective: To develop an effective leg recovery cycle and a powerful claw-back action via active ground contact

Description: This drill follows the High Knee and Butt Kicker drills, except that after the knee lift you extend the lower leg forward and then down. The aim is to cycle the leg as rapidly as possible. This movement is then followed by an active "pawing" of the ground, during which you emphasize pulling the ground underneath your body, thus contributing to ground forces. The pawing foot should land under the center of gravity to maximize the pushing forces and minimize any braking effect. The feeling is of stepping rapidly over a series of hurdles at approximately knee height. This drill can be performed in place, marching, skipping, or at full speed.

Figure 5-10

Coaching Points:

- The knee lift precedes all other movements.
- A rapid cycling of the leg into the extended position must take place.
- A pull-through action occurs at foot contact.
- Ground contact should be made under the center of gravity and on the balls of the feet.
- The athlete should "run tall" throughout the drill.
- Arm action must be coordinated with leg action.

Quick Feet (Figure 5-11)

Objective: To encourage a rapid leg turnover (cadence)

Description: Take as many steps as possible in a 5- to 10-yard space. Speed ladders or sticks can be a useful tool in quick-feet drills, but are by no means essential.

Figure 5-11

Coaching Points:

- Emphasize rapid leg turnover.
- Emphasize effective sprint mechanics.
- Ground contact should occur under the center of gravity and on the balls of the feet.
- Encourage light, rapid, and powerful ground contact.
- The foot should be dorsiflexed during the knee lift.
- Emphasize effective and coordinated arm action.

Hurdle Drill (Figure 5-12)

Objective: To develop an effective acceleration pattern of gradual stride lengthening, while also developing effective hip flexion

Description: Place mini-hurdles at increasing distances apart. Sprint over the hurdles while achieving a natural lengthening of the stride.

Figure 5-12

Coaching Points:

- The first strides must be short and rapid.

- Stride length must be increased while maintaining stride cadence.

- Stress the initial acceleration posture and action.

- Encourage light and rapid ground contact under the center of gravity and on the balls of the feet.

- Dorsiflexed foot action must occur during the knee lift.

- Encourage effective and coordinated arm action.

- The athletes run over the hurdles and do not jump.

Ankle-Action Development Drill

During sprinting, ground contact needs to be made with the balls of the feet. This action requires great strength and stability at the ankle joints. Straight-leg ankle flips are just one of a number of drills that can be performed to develop this active ankle action.

Ankling (Figure 5-13)

Objective: To encourage active ground contact via ankle dorsiflexion and use of the stretch–shorten cycle on contact

Description: Maintaining a practically straight leg action, propulsion is provided at the ankle joint. The foot is actively dorsiflexed as it leaves the ground and then actively plantarflexed on contact to develop force into the ground.

Figure 5-13

Coaching Points:

- Encourage straight-leg position.
- Remind the athletes to use small steps.
- Active dorsiflexion occurs as the foot leaves the ground.
- Powerful propulsion is provided by landing on the balls of the feet, utilizing the stretch–shorten cycle.
- Have the athletes focus on active ground contact.

Developing the Ability to Run Effectively at Optimal Speed

The aim at this stage is to transfer the techniques developed via the technique drills into enhanced running actions. Any technique session should always involve some speed runs so that the athlete can transfer the drill-based techniques into his running action. A quality speed-development program utilizes a variety of speed-running drills. Each drill works on a specific aspect of speed development, and their relative frequency of use depends upon the positional requirements and the individual player assessment.

Stationary starts—Stationary starts are traditional sprints, in which the athlete is required to sprint for a given distance from a stationary start. In soccer, a straight-ahead standing start is most common, but players also will be required to start to the side and backward. Therefore, these drills must also incorporate starts from the side and to the back as well as to the front (refer to Chapter 6 for optimal techniques).

Accelerative runs—The pattern in these drills is of a gradual acceleration (e.g., for a 60-yard sprint the pattern might be 20-yard stride, 20-yard faster, 20-yard fastest). The athlete is encouraged to "go through the gears" during the run. These runs are especially useful for athletes who need to reach maximum speed, as they can be performed without the fatigue of all-out effort over the accelerative period, thus increasing possible work output at maximum speed. These drills are also ideal for athletes who need to accelerate off a rolling start, as is often the case in soccer. In addition, acceleration drills can involve acceleration from an already high speed, during which a distinct change of speed is carried out at a given point.

Curvilinear runs—These runs are identical to the accelerative runs, except that they are carried out on curved courses. They replicate the types of running patterns players will take during the game, and again require acceleration from rolling starts. It is important to vary the direction of these runs so that the athlete is comfortable in working in all directions.

Ball drops—These drills are ideal for developing speed over short distances. A coach stands about five yards from the athlete with a tennis ball held in one hand. As the coach drops the ball, the athlete has to sprint to catch the ball before the second bounce. The distance can be increased as the athlete becomes more proficient, and two balls can be used to influence reaction time. Starts can be straight on, facing sideways, or facing backward, in which case a "go" command is given.

Ins and outs—These runs are used to contrast between running at maximum and submaximum speeds. Patterns can be changed to allow for sport specificity. The aim is to develop the ability to alternate between periods of maximum effort and periods during which speed is maintained but at a more cruising-type of level. This type of run is especially useful for soccer, because soccer athletes often need to cover a great deal of ground in a short time but do not want to be working at maximum effort the whole time.

"Ins" refers to periods of maximum effort and "outs" to more relaxed—but still fast—efforts. The emphasis during "ins" is to achieve maximum acceleration and speed, while on "outs" the aim is to run fast but relaxed.

Examples of ins and outs include a 60-yard sprint (20-yard ins, 20-yard outs, 20-yard ins), in which the athlete sprints flat-out for 20 yards, then runs relaxed for the following 20 yards, followed by a further acceleration and maximum effort for 20 yards. This run allows for the development of acceleration from both a stationary position and a rolling start. The out portion of the sprint can also be used to develop the athlete's ability to "cruise" at a high pace while using a relaxed sprinting action.

Sprint Loading

This work should only be introduced once a firm technique base has been established. The aim of sprint loading is to develop highly specific speed strength. It is based on overloading the sprint action to produce more explosive forces during the natural sprint action. Sprint-loading methods can include hill sprinting, sprinting with added weight, and towing sleds. Whichever method is utilized, it is vital at all times to ensure that distances and rest periods are appropriate to ensure that the athletes use their normal sprinting action. A modified action will negate any possible benefits of this type of training.

Hill sprinting—A low-grade hill (i.e., 8 to 10 degrees) and an appropriate distance must be used for the required adaptation. Similarly, rest periods should be scheduled to allow for full recovery. This type of hill sprinting must not be confused with that used for endurance training.

Added-weight sprints—Weight in the form of a weighted vest can be added to the body to provide an additional overload. Again, an appropriate level of resistance should be selected that does not alter sprint mechanics.

Towing (Figure 5-14)—Towing is possibly the most versatile method of sprint loading and can use resistance provided by sleds, partners, and rubber tubing. Again, an appropriate resistance should be selected. As a guideline, the athlete's speed should not be slowed by more that 10%. These methods also allow for contrast training. The resistance tubes also allow for sprint loading for multidirectional movements and can be applied to the agility drills outlined in Chapter 6.

Figure 5-14

Contrast Training

Contrast training provides an effective method of practicing sprint loading in which unresisted efforts are interspersed within the resisted efforts. For example, two resisted runs can be followed by an unresisted run, with the pattern repeated for the required number of runs. Contrast can also be provided within a run by releasing resistance. Contrast training allows for a more varied practice session and may contribute to enhanced learning and transfer.

Sample Sprint-Loading Progression

Figure 5-15 provides a sample sprint-loading progression. Resistance can be applied via a sled, a partner, or rubber tubing. Although intensity will be increased by adding resistance as the athlete's speed strength increases, at no time should the athlete be slowed by more than 10% of his maximum speed over the distance.

Week	Distance	Repetitions	Contrast Added
1	10	5	No
2	10	6	No
3	15	5	After sprint 2, 4
4	15	6	After sprint 3, 5
5	20	5	After sprint 2, 4
6	20	6	After sprint 2, 4, 6

Figure 5-15. Sprint loading progression

Sprint-Assisted Training

This method of training is introduced only with athletes with well-developed sprint techniques that stand up well in competitive situations. Also, the athletes should have a high level of speed strength.

The aim of sprint-assisted training is to provide a further speed overload by allowing the athlete to sprint at speeds over and above those of which he is currently capable. This method can develop both stride length and stride cadence. Methods of applying sprint-assisted training include downhill sprinting and towing.

As in sprint-resisted training, it is vital that the mechanics of the sprint are not altered during the application. When using sprint-assisted methods, the following safety aspects should govern the application of any overspeed training used.

- Sprint-assisted training should only be undertaken by athletes who have a strong background in speed training and have the necessary technique and speed strength to deal with this type of training.

- Sprint-assisted training should always be performed early in a session, following a thorough workout preparation (warm-up).

- Initial intensity and volume should be low to allow the athlete to adapt to this type of training.

  The most common methods of providing sprint-assisted speed are:

- Downhill sprinting

- Towing

Downhill Sprinting

The effectiveness of this type of training will depend on finding a suitable hill with a low grade, preferably a 3-degree slope. Ideally, a flat area will precede the hill to allow for acceleration to top speed, followed by a 15- to 30-yard downhill section and then another flat area. As hills like this are few and far between, common sense needs to prevail and sessions must be planned to maximize the effectiveness of any hill found.

Towing (Figure 5-16)

With the advent of various tubing and pulley systems, the application of overspeed training has become easier, allowing for more varied applications. These systems also allow for the application of overspeed to more soccer-specific movements such as

Figure 5-16

tracking shuffles and backpedals. The volume and intensity of the drills need to take into account both the nature of the athlete and the phase of training.

Runs should initially be low in volume (e.g., two to three repetitions, building to six to eight repetitions). They should also begin with a low distance (e.g., 10 yards) and then increase up to 30 to 40 yards.

The Importance of Speed Training

Speed is a skill and, hence, needs to be practiced. Therefore, while speed training will predominate at certain times (e.g., immediately preceding and during the main competition schedule), it is vital that some speed work is performed at all times, even in general preparatory work. Ideally, some sprint-technique work will be performed in every running or soccer session, as this repetition is needed to hone technique. Sprint drills provide an ideal medium for workout preparation and can be included in all sessions without encroaching on the time needed to be spent on other aspects of the game.

It must be remembered that speed is a neuromuscular skill and the speed pathways have to be constantly stimulated. If speed sessions are not included in a training program, these pathways will be neglected, potentially resulting in less than optimum speed development.

Session Organization

The organization of a speed session will vary with the setting in which it is delivered, and could well be incorporated into either general conditioning or soccer-based sessions. In some instances, coaches may conduct a dedicated speed session. In other cases, speed training may be linked with other variables such as agility or plyometrics. Speed training may also be part of a team's practice, in which a part of the session is dedicated to speed enhancement. Whatever the situation, it is vital that quality speed work is performed early in the session, when the athlete is fresh and is able to work at the required intensity to enhance speed. Ideally, soccer athletes should carry out at least one linear-based speed loading and one lateral-based (agility) loading per week.

For a full-speed session, the following session organization provides a logical order in which to place specific aspects of speed performance.

- *Workout preparation*, as covered in Chapter 4, precedes all sessions.
- The *innervation* aspect works on the need for rapid neural stimulation for sprinting. It utilizes rapid movements, but with an initially low amplitude, which increases as the warm-up continues. Quick-feet and ladder drills are useful at this time.

- During the *technical development phase*, specific aspects of sprint performance are developed while also continuing a warm-up toward maximum-effort sprints. Specific speed drills are selected to reflect the technical aspects to be worked on.

- The *maximum-speed phase* is where any maximum-speed and sprint-assisted work is carried out. Athletes will have undergone an effective warm-up, which will have stimulated the nervous system, and worked through an effective range of motion in preparation for this level of work, but without any fatigue having been developed. It is vital that all speed work is carried out in a nonfatigued state. The maximum-speed phase may involve linear work, lateral work, or combinations.

- Any *sprint-loading work*, such as resisted sprinting, should follow the maximum-speed work.

- Any *speed-endurance work* needs to be completed at the end of the session, or as a separate session of its own. This work should address the principal energy systems to be targeted.

- All sessions should be followed by a *cool-down*, during which the aim is to gradually return the body to a resting state. This cool-down is achieved via a gradual reduction in heart rate (elicited by a low-intensity level of activity), and a return of the working muscles to resting length via the stretch sequence laid out in Chapter 11.

6

Agility Training

Agility is a key factor in high-level soccer performance due to the varied movement requirements of the game, as outlined in Chapter 1, and the need to be able to read and react in both offensive and defensive situations. Agility involves a large number of movement requirements, including explosive changes in direction or speed, involving both accelerative and decelerative aspects; dynamic balance; and the ability to maintain coordinated movements under pressure from opposition. It can be seen to involve not only a power component, but also the ability to coordinate this power into smooth and effective movement. In addition, the concept of quickness is often included in discussions of agility. Quickness, in essence, involves the ability to read and react quickly and effectively to specific stimuli. Quickness, therefore, should be viewed as an integral part of agility.

Like speed, agility can be improved via training. To be optimally effective, the agility-development program needs to address all of the key movement requirements of elite soccer performance. When constructing agility programs, it is essential to deconstruct the movement requirements of soccer and individual positions, and identify movement skills and patterns required within a soccer match. Training programs and drills can then be generated to specifically address the movement demands of the game and the position.

Just as with speed development, agility training must not be done in isolation. It must be part of a multifaceted program that develops all of the aspects of superior performance. Effective agility depends on a sound base of strength and power, and on effective flexibility, balance, and movement patterns.

The Nature of Agility

Pure agility is extremely difficult to isolate, as it is intricately linked with a number of other parameters. When developing total agility for soccer, it is important to ensure that the following areas are addressed:

- Balance—both static and dynamic
- Reaction—ideally to sport-specific stimuli and multiple stimuli
- Accelerative ability—the ability to reach high speeds rapidly
- Decelerative ability—the ability to stop effectively and change movement appropriately
- Movement control—all movement is coordinated and controlled via appropriate movement patterns such as visual focus, body position, body movements, and footwork.

Movement Characteristics

When deconstructing soccer movements, it is important to look at the function of the movement as well as at the movement itself. For example, when looking at a side-shuffle movement, it is important to determine whether the aim is to get to a point as quickly as possible or to serve as a transition movement until the athlete is required to react to an external stimulus. This differentiation is vital, as the optimum technique in each of these situations will vary depending upon the aim of the movement. Aspects to consider when deconstructing movement requirements include the following:

- *Transition or actualization movement*—Is the movement performed in relative isolation or does it combine in any way with another movement? For example, does a backpedal occur by itself or is it followed by an action such as a jump? The answer to this question will determine the optimum technique (e.g., when the backpedal needs to be combined with a jump, it is imperative that the athlete keeps his body in a position from which a jump can be performed rapidly and effectively at any time).

- *Temporal factors*—At what speed does the movement occur? Remember, a situation could involve a combination of speeds.

- *Distances*—Over what distances do the specific movements occur? For example, backpedals are normally carried out over short distances, such as for a ball crossed just over a defender's head. For longer distances, such as a long ball played over the defender, the defender would be more effective drop-stepping and then running in a normal running pattern. Therefore, once basic movement patterns are established, drills should try to replicate soccer movements as closely as possible.

- *Reaction factors*—What is the nature of the stimulus? In soccer, the stimulus is usually ball or player movement. In terms of developing these areas, athletes should be asked to react to visual cues and not simply auditory cues.
- *Offensive or defensive*—Is the athlete dictating the nature of the movement combinations (i.e., offensive) or reacting to movements (i.e., defensive)? In soccer, players will need to develop abilities in both areas.

Fast Feet and Their Role in Agility

Many agility programs emphasize fast feet and an extensive use of tools like speed ladders. Fast feet (in multiple directions) certainly are vital in setting up an athlete for a fast reaction and in allowing optimum movement time. However, it is important to assess the contribution of fast feet to soccer-specific movements.

Fast feet, combined with the athletic position (discussed later in this chapter), place an athlete in an optimum position to react to a stimulus. However, once the athlete reacts, he then needs to move in the most effective way possible (e.g., to sprint for the ball). Once this reaction has taken place, a move is made into a different movement pattern (e.g., a sprint acceleration). Therefore, when constructing drills it is important to combine multiple movement patterns and not focus solely on fast-feet drills. The key to all of the agility drills is to keep the athlete in a position from which he can accelerate.

Areas of Focus

When coaching optimum agility technique the following areas of focus need to be examined.

The feet—Appropriate foot contact varies with the movement pattern being carried out. For general movement patterns and fast-feet drills, light ground contact is essential and must be taught. Similarly, the dorsiflexed (toe up) position must be stressed at all times. The feet should be placed perpendicular to the direction of movement, with the weight on the balls of the feet rather than the toes. However, when planting the foot to cut, for example, the foot should be placed flat (but with the weight generally on the balls of the feet) to allow for greater ground-contact time and the generation of the greatest forces.

The ankles—As in speed development, effective movement depends upon the effective use of the energy generated via the stretch–shorten cycle. Therefore, the ankles must be trained to utilize this energy source. Again, the dorsiflexed position is essential for effective movement.

The linear and lateral muscles—In linear speed work, the drive muscles (i.e., quadriceps, glutes, and hamstrings) that generate linear motion dominate and need effective speed-strength characteristics. Lateral movement, on the other hand, requires an athlete to shuffle, cross-step, drop-step, and cut, among other movements. Therefore, emphasis must also be placed on the muscles that generate these movements (e.g., glutes, adductors, and abductors).

The torso—Quick movement originates at the hips, and this fact must be stressed in the performance of agility drills. The hips are the steering wheel of the body and therefore must be a key focus for agility development. It is essential that a high degree of mobility is maintained at the hips. In addition, effective movement requires a strong and stable base, which is provided by a strong torso musculature. Core strength can provide the stable platform from which all other movements are generated (refer to Chapter 9).

The head—The head should always remain in line with the spine. The eyes should be kept level and should initiate movement together with the hips by indicating the direction of movement. This alignment allows for a high level of movement control.

The neuromuscular system—The neuromuscular system must be a primary focus of training. The aim must be to teach the muscles to fire quickly and carry out movements at rapid speeds, with the movement patterns replicating those required in soccer as closely as possible.

The Athletic Position

Effective movement in soccer depends upon the ability to read and react to a stimulus and then move efficiently and effectively in response. The cornerstone of this ability is putting the body in a position from which it can effectively move in any required direction without the need for any countermovements that may slow total movement. The athletic position, as shown in Figures 6-1 and 6-2, is the cornerstone of the majority

Figure 6-1

Figure 6-2

of the agility drills in this chapter. A key to the athletic position is the production of positive angles, which need to be generated at the ankles, knees, and hips. These angles place the body in a position in which it is "loaded" for action. These positive angles need to be applied within an effective base of support to provide the stable platform from which effective movement can be initiated.

Structuring the Agility-Development Plan

Any agility-development program should fit into a long-term plan, with a base of simple closed-movement skills, gradually building to complex open skills once the basics are mastered. Thus, both short- and long-term goals need to be set with the aim of developing efficient and effective movement skills. Each session should have a specific goal, and activities should be planned that contribute to that goal. It is vital that drills are carefully planned and not just thrown together. Remember, it is impossible to target every skill in every workout. Technical correctness is crucial, and so the focus should be on quality, not quantity. The use of appropriate feedback cues can assist in the correct performance of the drills.

The Agility Pyramid

The agility pyramid has been constructed to take into account all of the ideal learning factors outlined in Chapter 2. This development sequence ensures that the following key elements of agility development are addressed:

- The initial development of basic movement patterns
- Appropriate progression from simple to complex skills
- Appropriate progression from closed to open skills

Base program—The base program develops the key basic skills, including achieving the athletic position, developing body control while moving, and developing the key movement patterns. It is important that the athlete spends time mastering these basic movements, as they form the foundation upon which all agility is subsequently built.

Development program—This stage further develops the basic skills addressed in the base program via the use of increasingly challenging closed-agility drills. Toward the later part of this stage, open drills are introduced.

Peak program—The peak program involves high-quality closed drills and very soccer-specific open drills that develop the ability to read, react, and move efficiently in response to soccer-specific stimuli.

The Basic Movements

While initially the movement requirements for soccer appear complex, a number of key movement patterns can be identified, with the overall patterns of movement seen in a game being the combination of these basic patterns, which therefore provide the cornerstone of the entire agility program. It is essential that these movements are practiced extensively and mastered prior to an athlete moving on to the more complex drills.

Controlled Backpedals (Figure 6-3)

Objective: To develop the ability to move backward while keeping the body in an athletic position from which it can react to any stimulus

Description: Run backward over a given distance (5 to 10 yards) in a controlled fashion.

Figure 6-3

Coaching Points:

- It is vital to ensure that the bodyweight is forward at all times.
- Positive angles must be achieved at the hips, knees, and ankles.
- Encourage the athletes to make short, rapid strides.
- The center of gravity must be kept low.

Note: This drill allows for an effective transition from backward movement to a sideways, forward, or jumping movement if and when required.

Rapid Backpedals (Figure 6-4)

Objective: To cover a short distance very quickly while facing forward (This movement is not used as often as the controlled backpedal.)

Description: The athlete covers a given distance (five to 10 yards) as quickly as possible by backpedaling.

Figure 6-4

Coaching Points:

* The body is a little more upright than in the Controlled Backpedals drill, but should never be fully upright.
* The center of gravity should be higher than in the Controlled Backpedals drill.
* Longer strides are to be taken than in the Controlled Backpedals drill.

Note: In a game, this action will normally end with a jump or similar action that requires the athlete to move into a more athletic position toward the end of the drill.

Side-Shuffle (Figures 6-5 and 6-6)

Objective: To develop an effective and controlled side-shuffle technique, together with lateral accelerative and decelerative ability

Description: Set up two lines five to 10 yards apart. Move from line 1 to line 2, back to line 1, and so on, utilizing a side-shuffle motion.

Coaching Points:

* The movement should be a series of short sideward steps, and not a series of skips.

Figure 6-5

Figure 6-6

- The athletic position should be maintained at all times, as this puts the body in a position to react to any stimulus rapidly and effectively.
- The body should never become upright.
- Each foot should be placed almost flat with the weight forward on the ball of the foot.
- The feet should be at right angles to the direction of movement at all times.

Cross-Step (Figures 6-7, 6-8, and 6-9)

Objective: To develop the ability to accelerate effectively in a lateral direction. The cross-step is the most effective way of accelerating laterally and must be mastered prior to moving into other drills.

Description: Stand with your feet facing forward. Moving to the left, rotate the hips left and then drive the right leg powerfully across the body, thereby putting yourself in a good accelerative position. The initial hip rotation is a vital aspect of the cross-step, as this action allows for a far more fluid cross-step with a far more efficient range of motion. From this point, you can quickly move into the normal acceleration-running action.

Coaching Points:

- This movement is initiated with a hip rotation, with the head also leading the action.
- The foot should start to pivot with this rotation.
- The far knee should drive up and across the body.
- This foot should be driven down into the ground.
- A vigorous sprint-acceleration action should follow.

Figure 6-7   Figure 6-8   Figure 6-9

Drop-Step (Figures 6-10, 6-11, and 6-12)

Objective: To develop an optimum technique for rapid acceleration to the rear

Description: Stand facing forward. While rotating (opening) the hips to the right, take a diagonal step back with the right foot (when moving to the right). Follow this movement with a powerful cross-step with the left leg and accelerate away. This action allows for a rapid transition into the normal linear acceleration pattern.

Figure 6-10   Figure 6-11   Figure 6-12

Coaching Points:

- This movement is initiated with an opening of the hips (the hips and head lead the action).
- No false steps should take place.
- A powerful diagonal step is taken, with the opposite foot in a pivot position.
- The far leg then initiates a powerful drive up and across the body.
- An effective sprint-acceleration technique should then be utilized.

The Track (Figures 6-13 and 6-14)

Objective: To track an attacking player while keeping the body in a position from which it can react in either direction

Description: Run backward over a given distance while keeping the body at a 45-degree angle. Every two or three strides, rotate the body left and right as if tracking an attacker's movements.

Figure 6-13   Figure 6-14

Coaching Points:

- Short compact steps should be taken.
- Have the players use a combination of side-shuffle steps, running steps and drop-steps.
- Instruct the player to switch left and right throughout the drill.
- The body weight must remain forward and the athletic position must be maintained.
- Remind the athletes that the hips control the movement.

The Cut (Figures 6-15 and 6-16)

Objective: To develop the key movement for changing direction

Description: Place a series of poles five yards apart at a 45-degree angle. Run through the line, changing directions at each pole via an effective cut.

Figure 6-15   Figure 6-16

Coaching Points:

- At the point of direction change, the foot should be planted wide and parallel to the body.
- The foot should land flat, but with the body weight forward on the ball of the foot.
- The foot should land outside the knee to allow for effective force production.
- The athlete should then powerfully push off this foot in the direction he wants to move.

Note: While cones are commonly used for marking out agility areas, the use of poles is recommended for some drills, as poles requires a greater degree of accuracy and better replicate the nature of on-field agility.

The Chop-Step (Figure 6-17)

Objective: To effectively change speed and/or direction. The chop-step puts the body in an effective position for decelerating, reacting to opponents' moves, and initiating offensive moves, and therefore must be an integral part of any direction change.

Description: Approach a cone with a normal running action. At the cone, dramatically shorten your strides using quick feet–type movements with the feet wider than normal.

Also, drop the center of gravity and achieve an effective forward lean at the hips. This action creates an effective athletic position from which to react and or initiate other movements.

Figure 6-17

Coaching Point:

• Positive angles must be achieved at the hips, knees, and ankles.

Note: Once this skill is mastered, it is developed in the later phases by adding tasks to perform a given movement after the chop-step (e.g., chop-step and change direction).

The Bounce (Figure 6-18)

Objective: To utilize the stretch–shorten cycle to enable an effective and efficient reaction to any stimulus

Description: From an athletic position, actively and rapidly bounce on the balls of the feet, but without any significant rise in the body position.

Coaching Points:

• The bounce is on the balls of the feet.

• The bounce is rapid but of low height.

• The athletic position must be maintained throughout the drill.

Figure 6-18

Closed Development Drills

The aim of closed development drills is to develop the basic techniques via a progressive series of different types of drills in which the basic movement patterns are combined. The drills are initially closed, but the read and react aspects are introduced toward the end of the phase.

These drills can involve a huge variety of different movement patterns and the drills outlined in this section are only a small sample of those available. The aim of all of these drills is to enable the athlete to further develop the key movement patterns developed in the base phase in increasingly challenging situations that progressively combine movements and move from closed to open drills. The coach should aim to combine movement patterns that are common in soccer.

The focus should always be on technique. A key to success in this area is how well the athlete is able to carry out effective transitions between different movements. The athlete must always keep himself in a position from which he can accelerate, both when moving (via correct movement patterns) and stationary (via the bounce technique).

Sprint Loading

As with speed work, loading can be added to agility drills via the use of elastic resistance. Similar guidelines need to be followed as for speed work (i.e., resistance should not affect technique). Contrast-type training can also be utilized during the performance of these drills.

Closed Agility Drills

ZIGZAG DRILLS

The Zigzag Cut (Figure 6-19)

Objective: To develop the cutting action

Description: Set up six cones five yards apart and offset by five yards.

- Sprint from the start to cone A.
- Chop-step and then cut, sprinting off to cone B.
- Repeat this action to all six cones.

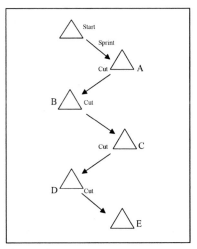

Figure 6-19

79

Zigzag Shuffle and Sprint (Figure 6-20)

Objective: To develop the ability to move from a side-shuffle to a sprint

Description: Five cones laid out five yards apart and offset five yards.

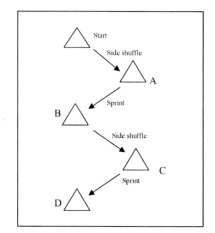

- Side shuffle from the start to cone A.

- Sprint to cone B.

- Side shuffle to cone C.

- Sprint to cone D.

Figure 6-20

Coaching Points:

- A good athletic position must be maintained through the side shuffle.

- False steps should be minimized during transitions.

- Quick steps must be taken during the acceleration.

Zigzag Backpedal and Sprint (Figure 6-21)

Objective: To develop the ability to move from a backpedal to a sprint via an effective cross-step

Description: Five cones are laid out five yards apart and offset five yards.

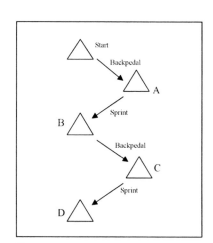

- Backpedal from the start to cone A.

- Cross-step and sprint to cone B.

- Backpedal to cone C.

- Cross-step and sprint to cone D.

Figure 6-21

Coaching Points:

- A good athletic position must maintained throughout the backpedal.

- An effective cross-step should be used.

- False steps should be minimized during transitions.

- Quick steps must be taken during the acceleration.

BAG DRILLS

Bag Sprint, Shuffle, and Backpedal (Figure 6-22)

Objective: To develop the ability to move from a sprint to a side shuffle to a backpedal

Description: Six bags are laid out five yards apart.

- Sprint from the start to the end of bag 1.
- Side shuffle along side of bag 1.
- Backpedal along bag 2.
- Side shuffle along the side of bag 2.
- Sprint forward along bag 3.
- Carry on through the bags.

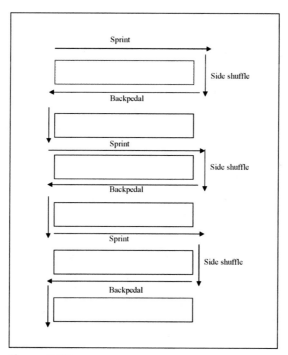

Figure 6-22

Coaching Points:

- A good athletic position must be maintained throughout the drill.
- False steps should be minimized during transitions.

Bag Sprint and Shuffle (Figure 6-23)

Objective: To develop the ability to move from a sprint to a side shuffle to a sprint

Description: Six bags are laid out five yards apart.

- Sprint from the start to the end of bag 1.
- Side shuffle along side of bag 1.
- Drop-step and sprint along bag 2.
- Side shuffle along the side of bag 2.
- Drop-step and sprint forward along bag 3.
- Carry on through the bags.

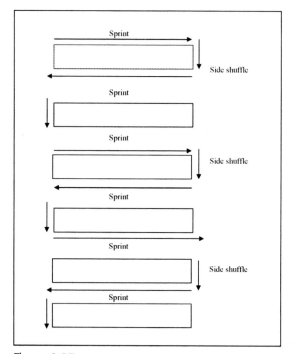

Figure 6-23

Coaching Points:

- A good athletic position must be maintained throughout the drill.
- Effective drop-steps must be used.
- False steps should be minimized during transitions.

Bag Side Shuffle and Backpedal (Figure 6-24)

Objective: To develop the ability to side shuffle rapidly

Description: Six bags are laid out five yards apart.

- Side shuffle from the start to the end of bag 1.
- Sprint along the side of bag 1.
- Side shuffle along bag 2.
- Sprint along the side of bag 2.
- Carry on through the bags.

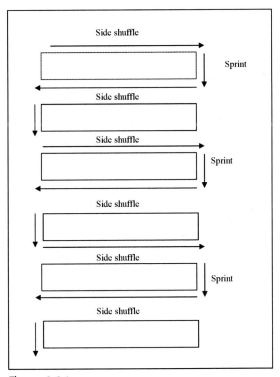

Figure 6-24

Coaching Points:

- A good athletic position must be maintained throughout the drill.
- False steps should be minimized during transitions.

CONE DRILLS

Cone Sprint, Side Shuffle, Backpedal, and Side Shuffle (Figure 6-25)

Objective: To develop key movement patterns and transitions between movements

Description: Set up four cones in a 5- x 5-yard square.

- Sprint forward from cone A to cone B.
- Side shuffle to cone C.
- Backpedal to cone D
- Shuffle to cone A.

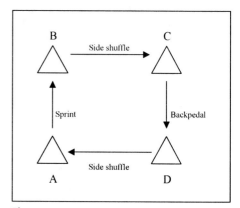

Figure 6-25

Coaching Points:

- A good athletic position must be maintained throughout the drill.
- False steps should be minimized during transitions.

Side Shuffle, Sprint, Side Shuffle, and Sprint (Figure 6-26)

Objective: To develop key movement patterns and transitions between movements

Description: Four cones are set up in a 5- x 5-yard square.

- Facing into the grid, side shuffle from cone A to cone B.
- Sprint forward to cone C.
- Side shuffle to cone D (facing outward).
- Drop-step and sprint to cone A.

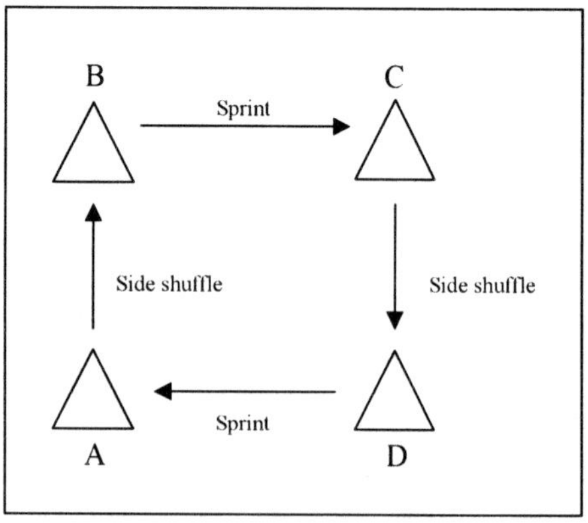

Figure 6-26

Coaching Points:

- A good athletic position must be maintained throughout the drill.
- False steps should be minimized during transitions.
- Effective drop-steps must be used.

Sprint. Backpedal, Sprint, Backpedal, Sprint (Figure 6-27)

Objective: To develop key movement patterns and transitions between movement

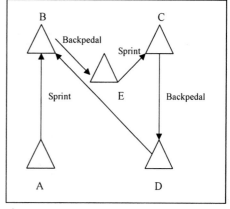

Figure 6-27

Description: Four cones are set up in a 5- x 5-yard square, with a fifth cone in the center of the square.

- Sprint from cone A to cone B.

- Backpedal to cone E.

- Sprint to cone C.

- Backpedal to cone D.

- Sprint to cone B.

Coaching Points:

- A good athletic position must be maintained throughout the drill.

- False steps should be minimized during transitions.

- Effective chop-steps must be used.

90-Degree Cut and Go (Figure 6-28)

Objective: To develop an attacker's ability to run across the offside line before accelerating forward

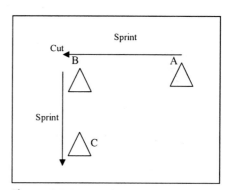

Figure 6-28

Description: Set up two cones (A and B) 10 yards apart, with a third cone (C) at a 90-degree angle from cone B and 10 yards away.

- Sprint from cone A to cone B.

- Cut and sprint forward to cone C.

Coaching Points:

- A good athletic position must be maintained throughout the drill.

- Effective transitions must be used.

- A chop-step must be used prior to the direction change.

Note: This drill can be varied by changing the run-off angle, which can vary up to 180 degrees in both directions. The athlete should vary the initial run to replicate runs used in a game. Some runs will involve a simultaneous cut and speed change.

90-Degree Turn and Go (Figure 6-29)

Objective: To develop an attacker's ability to run across the offside line before accelerating

Description: Set up two cones (A and B) 10 yards apart, with a third cone (C) at a 90-degree angle from cone B and 10 yards away.

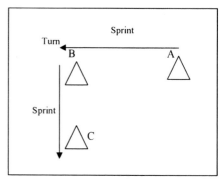

Figure 6-29

- Sprint from cone A to cone B.
- Turn tightly around cone B before sprinting forward to cone C.

Coaching Points:

- A good athletic position must be maintained throughout the drill.
- Effective transitions must be used.
- A chop-step must be used prior to the direction change.

Note: This drill can be varied by changing the run-off angle, which can vary up to 180 degrees in both directions. The athlete should vary the initial run to replicate runs used in a game. Some runs will involve a simultaneous turn and speed change.

Y Pattern Backpedal and Go (Figure 6-30)

Objective: To replicate a defensive situation in which the defender is backpedaling and waiting to respond to an attacker's move

Description: Set up two cones (A and B) 10 yards apart and two additional cones (C and D) at 45-degree angles and 10 yards away from cone B to the left and right.

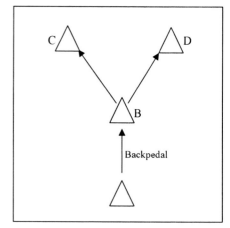

Figure 6-30

- Backpedal from cone A to cone B.
- On the coach's command, drop-step and then sprint off to your left or right.

Coaching Points:

- A good athletic position must be maintained throughout the drill.
- Effective transitions must be used.

Y Pattern Track and Go (Figure 6-31)

Objective: To replicate a defensive situation in which the defender is tracking an attacker's moves and waiting to respond to the attacker's key move

Description: Set up two cones (A and B) 10 yards apart, and two additional cones (C and D) at 45-degree angles and 10 yards away from cone B to the left and right.

*   Track from cone A to cone B.

*   On the coach's command, sprint off to your left or right.

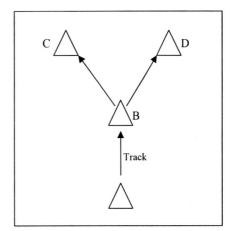

Figure 6-31

Coaching Points:

*   A good athletic position must be maintained throughout the drill.

*   Effective transitions must be used.

Three-Corner Sprint (Figure 6-32)

Objective: To develop acceleration, deceleration, and turning ability

Description: Set up four cones in an 8- x 8-yard square.

*   Sprint from cone A to cone B.

*   Touch cone B and sprint to cone C.

*   Touch cone C and sprint to cone D.

Coaching Points:

*   A good athletic position must be maintained throughout the drill.

*   Effective transitions must be used.

*   Chop-steps should be used prior to any direction change.

Note: This drill can also be performed by running around poles at B and C.

The Weave (Figure 6-33)

Objective: To develop effective dodging and weaving movements

Descriptions: Lay out a series of poles or cones at different distances and positions. The poles can be set out in different alignments to add both variety and specificity to the drill. Sprint through the poles while maintaining your speed and using effective movement patterns. This drill can also be combined with other drills, such as dribbling a ball. Other athletes can be added to the drill by running in a different direction. Doing so increases the difficulty of the drill, as the runners need to avoid each other as well as the poles.

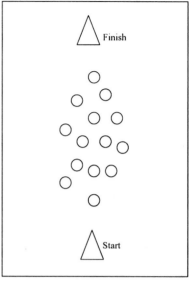

Figure 6-33

Coaching Points:

- A good athletic position must be maintained throughout the drill.
- Effective transitions must be used.
- Ensure that sufficient rest is given between runs to preserve movement quality.

Sprint and React (Figure 6-34)

Objective: To develop the ability to chop-step and then react and sprint

Description: Set up two cones (A and B) 10 yards apart and five colored cones in a semicircle 5 yards away from cone B.

- Sprint form cone A to cone B.
- Chop-step before reaching cone B.
- Sprint off to the appropriate cone on the coach's command.

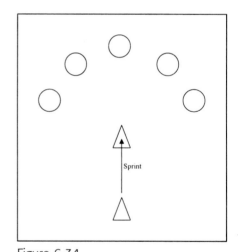

Figure 6-34

Coaching Points:

- A good athletic position must be maintained throughout the drill.
- Effective transitions must be used.
- A chop-step should be used prior to any direction change.
- Make sure an effective acceleration pattern is used.

Open Drills

Open drills are used with athletes who have mastered the basic movement patterns of the base phase and can combine them effectively into the closed drills of the development phase. The aim at this point is to develop these basic agility skills into the specific movement requirements of soccer. Sessions at this stage should show an increasing quality in the performance of the development drills and the use of more random/open drills. The athletes' focus should become increasingly soccer-related. It is the coach's hope that the movement patterns developed in the previous phases are so engrained that movement is efficient and effective without the need to focus on the actual movement pattern. This ability allows the focus to shift externally to the task at hand, just as it would in a game. The key points in all of these drills are the maintenance of the basic movement patterns and their effective integration into efficient and effective open movements.

Get Behinds (Figure 6-35)

One player stands facing a partner. He attempts to get behind his partner as the partner attempts to keep him from doing so. The emphasis should be on rapid foot movement while the body remains in the athletic position. This drill simulates marking in tight situations.

Figure 6-35

Shark in the Tank (Figure 6-36)

This drill is essentially a game of tag, but at a high intensity. Mark out a grid 10 yards by 10 yards. Three or four players should be in the square. One player sprints into the grid and attempts to tag all of the players in the time allotted, which should be short (i.e., less than five seconds). The focus must remain on the quality of movement.

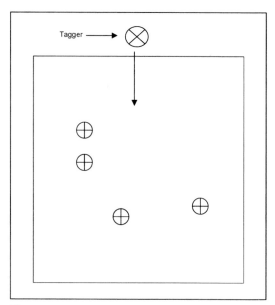

Figure 6-36

Partner Chase (Figure 6-37)

In a given area, one partner attempts to get away from the other in the time allotted, while the other attempts to stay as close as possible. A Velcro™ belt can be used as a visual cue.

In addition, the offensive athlete can be given a specific area he has to reach. This variation develops the ability to initially lead the defender away from the target in an attempt to create space, which is a useful skill in soccer. This drill simulates close marking situations, such as in the penalty box and on corners.

Figure 6-37

The Track (Figures 6-38 and 6-39)

This is a very soccer-specific drill that builds on the tracking steps developed in the base phase. Mark out a channel. The defender stands three yards inside the channel and the attacker enters the grid. The attacker aims to use effective cuts to run past the defender, who attempts to track the attacker by keeping the feet moving effectively and by keeping the body in a good athletic position to be able to react to any move of the attacker. A wide variety of distances and angles can be used to match the varied requirements of soccer. Variety can be added via the direction of the athletes entering the grid and also by the instructions given (e.g., a defender aims to make a tag in the right half of the grid, requiring him to force the attacker in a set direction).

Figure 6-38

Figure 6-39

Wall Reactions (Figure 6-40)

This drill develops reaction abilities while stressing the importance of maintaining the athletic position at all times. One athlete faces a wall from a distance of five to 10 yards. The partner throws a soccer ball against the wall and the athlete tries to control it appropriately (e.g., header, chest, knee, foot). The drill can be made more difficult by moving the athlete closer to the wall. It is important that the athlete maintains an athletic position and loads the muscles by using a "bounce" on the balls of the feet.

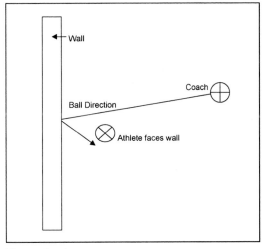

Figure 6-40

The Session

Agility sessions may be totally devoted to agility or may represent a small part of a larger session. Therefore, no definitive rules can be provided regarding how an agility session should be run. For example, coaches often use agility drills in warm-ups prior to technical sessions. However, the following guidelines provide an appropriate structure for high-quality agility sessions.

Workout preparation: This aspect is covered in Chapter 4.

Innervation: Stimulate the neural pathways through the use of fast-feet drills such as ladder work, with lateral drills dominating.

Mechanics: As the emphasis is on developing agility, agility mechanics will dominate, as opposed to linear mechanics, which dominate speed sessions. Drills should feature predominantly closed movements until basic mechanics have been developed.

Movement drills: These drills are used to develop basic techniques into soccer-related movements. Progress from closed to open movements. Resisted and assisted movements can be utilized in these practices.

Power practices: Any plyometric work can be carried out in these sessions.

Endurance work: Endurance work is carried out at the end of the session, emphasizing the key energy system selected.

Cool-down: The aim of a cool-down is to gradually return the body to a resting state, via a gradual reduction in heart rate (elicited by a low-intensity level of activity), and to return the working muscles to resting length using the stretching sequence outlined in Chapter 11.

The relative time spent in each section will vary by athlete. Beginner athletes will spend the greatest time on basic mechanics. Experienced athletes will spend more time on movement drills, with increasingly complex movements requiring reactions to increasing stimuli under increasingly random situations.

7

Strength Training

No soccer player can hope to perform at his optimal level unless he undertakes a well-designed program of resistance training. Strength and power underpin so many aspects of performance that unless they are well-developed, performance will be compromised. Setting up a program requires a fundamental understanding of the scientific principles underlying strength performance and of what the resistance program is trying to achieve.

Key Definitions

Strength training is a term that encapsulates many methodologies. To maximize the effect of any training program, it is important to determine the exact requirement of the strength-training program. A number of key terms used in this text are defined in this section to ensure full understanding of the aims of the program.

Maximal strength—The maximal force that a muscle or muscle group can generate in a given position at a given velocity. This term also refers to the maximal force-production capability of the body.

Peak force—The maximal force that can be exerted in a specific situation. For soccer, peak force could involve the ability to generate force rapidly during a jump or a sprint. It is important that any force capability generated by the program is transferred into the specific actions required on the soccer field.

Relative strength—Strength expressed in relation to the player's body weight. While some athletes need to increase their body weight, for others the aim of the strength-training program will be an increase in force capability without any increase in mass. This difference in goals needs to be considered when setting up the program.

Power—The "time rate of doing work," measured as force x distance/time. In many instances in soccer, the ability to exert forces rapidly is crucial, such as in running, jumping, and shooting.

Hypertrophy—An increase in the size of existing muscle fibers. Hypertrophy can take the form of myofibrillar hypertrophy, which is an increase in size of the contractile elements of the fiber, or sarcoplasmic hypertrophy, which is an increase in cell volume. Athletic conditioning should aim to ensure that the former represents the greatest degree of hypertrophy.

Repetition—The movement of the weight from the start position of an exercise to the midpoint and back to the start. Repetitions are the basic building blocks of all resistance exercises.

Set—A given number of repetitions (e.g., if an athlete completes a sequence of six repetitions, he has completed one set of six repetitions).

Motoneuron—A nerve cell innervating muscle cells.

Motor unit—A motoneuron and the muscle cells it innervates.

Fast-twitch fibers—Muscle fibers that are characterized by high force capacity, a high rate of force development, and low endurance. These fibers can be either Type IIA or Type IIB.

Slow-twitch fibers—Muscle fibers that are characterized by low force capacity, low rate of force development, and high endurance.

Types of Muscular Work

During any muscular work, three types of muscle action are evident that contribute differently to soccer performance. Understanding their influence will help is designing appropriate programs.

Concentric—Work carried out when a muscle shortens. Concentric work is normally associated with the lifting portion of resistance training.

Isometric—Muscle action whereby no shortening or lengthening occurs. Isometric work occurs when a weight is held in position. Isometric strength is normally 20 percent greater than concentric strength.

Eccentric—Muscle lengthening, which occurs when a weight is lowered with control. Eccentric strength is normally 40 percent greater than concentric strength. To maximize the use of this contraction, weights should be lowered with control in many of the strength exercises.

Force/Velocity Relationships

High force output requires time to be produced. Therefore, high force outputs tend to occur at slow velocities, meaning that pure strength is important in these situations. Traditional heavy resistance training is the best way to developing this strength. Therefore, strength programs should focus on controlled speed of lifting, emphasizing both the concentric (lifting) and eccentric (lowering) phases of the exercises. Strength is best developed with high resistances that affect predominantly fast-twitch muscle fibers, utilizing low repetitions (i.e., three to six). Rest between sets should be sufficient to allow for maximal forces in subsequent sets.

However, many situations in soccer, such as sprinting and changing directions, require that force be developed rapidly, and are therefore dependent upon the rate of force development (i.e., how quickly forces are produced), rather than simply on maximal force capacity.. Thus, for many playing positions, power will be the key element to develop. In the initial stages of training, increases in strength will increase power, meaning that the early phases of training should focus on strength development. However, as a player's strength increases, strength training alone will not increase power. At this point, explosive movements are needed. Explosive exercises are based on Olympic weightlifting movements and their derivatives, as well as many of the basic exercises (e.g., squats, bench press) performed explosively. The Olympic movements require both excellent technique and a solid strength base.

Peak power output comes at different resistances for different exercises (i.e., 40 to 85 percent of 1 RM). To facilitate this variation, a range of resistances must be utilized during the power-training phase, along with traditional heavier resistances. Rest between sets should be sufficient to allow for maximal power output in subsequent sets. A moderate number of sets (three to six) should be performed utilizing low repetitions, with the quality of work being more important than the quantity. In all explosive exercises, once the movement power starts to decline, the set should be terminated.

Muscle Hypertrophy

Today's soccer players are bigger than ever before, and therefore need a higher level of muscle hypertrophy. The level of development needed is dependent upon the playing position. Therefore, a certain degree of muscle hypertrophy should be a goal for all athletes and a major aim for players whose future performance may be negatively affected by a lack of physical presence. To achieve peak hypertrophy, a higher volume of training is needed, with an emphasis on higher repetitions (i.e., eight to 12), and with a shorter rest period between sets than in the strength- and power-development sessions.

Training Effects

A training session and program will have a number of effects on the body. These effects need to be considered when designing the program.

Acute effects—Effects that occur during the exercise session (e.g., an increase in blood supply, a reduction in force capacity).

Immediate effects—Effects that occur immediately after the cessation of an exercise session. In general, the overall effect of any training session is a short-term reduction in performance, as fatigue generally is greater than any potentiation effects. This result is to be expected, and should not be a cause for concern.

Cumulative effects—The combined effects of a number of training sessions (i.e., the program). These effects are the stimulus for improved performance. Training should always be thought of as a long-term process. Optimal performance takes a long period of time to develop, and short-term approaches are seldom effective.

Delayed effects—Effects that manifest themselves at a given time after a training session. Many of the full performance-enhancing effects of training will only fully manifest themselves after a period of time, especially when residual fatigue is negated. This response is fundamental to the ability to peak at a given time.

Residual effects—The changes that are retained beyond the timescale normally associated with adaptation. Some fitness variables take longer to decay than others, and this can help influence the periodization plans outlined in Chapter 14. Training needs to take a long-term approach to optimally engage this principle.

Partial effects—The changes that occur as a result of a single exercise within a workout (e.g., squats).

Adaptations to Training

The way a body adapts to a period of training is quite complex and involves an number of physiological systems. Adaptation to a training program can be seen in the following systems:

- Muscular system
- Neural system
- Hormonal system

Muscular System

These adaptations are traditionally associated with resistance training. The muscles can be thought of as the computer hardware that performs key tasks. Adaptations to the muscular system include the following:

- Increased muscle hypertrophy, especially in fast-twitch fibers
- Conversion of Type IIB to Type IIA muscle fibers
- An increase in the strength of connective tissue, including ligaments, tendons, and the connective tissue surrounding muscles

Neural System

Effective strength and power performance also depends upon the neural system. The muscles will only work optimally when they are appropriately activated. If the muscular system is the hardware, the neural system is the software needed for optimal functioning. Neural system adaptations to a period of resistance training affect both intra- and intermuscular coordination.

Intramuscular adaptations include:

- Recruitment of an increased number of motor units, increasing the force capacity
- Optimal rate coding, increasing the firing rate of the muscles
- An increase in motor-unit synchronicity, allowing the muscles to work together effectively to produce effective movement

Intermuscular coordination adaptations include:

- An improved coordination of muscle actions, allowing for effective technique development
- Enhanced force-transference capacity between body segments, allowing for optimal expression of force

All of these neural adaptations taken together mean that significant strength increases can take place without any muscle hypertrophy. This statement is especially important if the aim of the program is to increase relative strength, but avoid an increase in body mass.

Hormonal System

Hormonal adaptations result in an increased quantity and activity of key anabolic hormones. Hormones, such as testosterone, are vital for effective muscle growth. When hypertrophy is needed, programs that optimally stimulate hormonal adaptations are required. Therefore, the training methods used for developing muscle hypertrophy differ from those aiming at maximal strength development. These differences are reflected in the guidelines given in this chapter.

Muscle-Fiber Recruitment

Muscle-fiber recruitment happens according to two key principles:

- All or none principle
- Principle of orderly recruitment

All or None Principle

Muscular force is controlled by the number of motor units recruited, not by the force output of individual motor units. A motor unit is either active or inactive. Therefore, if a submaximal force output is required, the number of motor units recruited will be sufficient to produce that force. For full force output, the maximal number of motor units needs to be recruited. Recruiting increasing numbers of fibers and increasing the force-producing capacity of each fiber are two of the key aims of training.

Principle of Orderly Recruitment

Motor-unit recruitment takes a stepwise approach, with slow-twitch fibers recruited first, followed by type IIA and then IIB. The number of units recruited is controlled by the force requirements of the movement. Only high-force movements can recruit the key Type II fibers that generate the greatest force and power output. All movements are thought to follow the principle of orderly recruitment, although some research suggests that ballistic-type movements can selectively recruit Type IIB fibers. It is important that resistances are selected that allow for the development of fast-twitch muscle fibers.

Designing the Program

Soccer movements involve multijoint, multiplanar movements, with the force generated by the major lower-body mobilizer muscles. Movements tend to be short and emphasize high power outputs. Resistance training for soccer needs to be specific to the needs of the game, and to the requirements of the athlete concerned. The programs presented in this section are based on the following guidelines:

Training movements not muscles—Training must emphasize the development of soccer performance and train movements that are common in soccer. Soccer training should not follow bodybuilding-program patterns in which individual muscles are emphasized, often via isolation exercises. Instead, it must develop the key movement-patterns needs for soccer.

Multijoint movements—Exercises such as squats involve movement at a number of joints, utilize a number of muscles, and stimulate the greatest strength and hypertrophy gains. These exercises should take precedence over single-joint movements, and they are the fundamental building blocks of the programs in this book.

Multiplanar movements—Soccer movements involve a number of planes of motion, and strength needs to be developing in all planes for optimal effectiveness. The programs outlined in this book develop multiplanar strength.

Ground-based exercise—In soccer, force is predominantly generated with the feet in contact with the ground. The resistance-training program should therefore utilize ground-based exercises.

Free weights—Free-weight exercises stimulate the stabilization functions of the body and are preferred over machine-based resistance, which normally has a fixed movement track and requires little stabilization and balance development.

Methods of Strength Training

Methods of strength training can be classified in terms of the methods utilized to achieve maximal muscular tension, which is required to produce the adaptations to strength training highlighted earlier in this chapter. In general, three ways exist to generate maximal muscular tension:

- *Maximal-effort method*—Lifting a maximal load
- *Repeated-effort method*—Lifting a submaximal load to failure, thereby achieving maximum muscular tension in a fatigued state
- *Dynamic-effort method*—Lifting a submaximal load with maximal velocity

Maximal-Effort Method

This method, which is superior for developing both inter- and intramuscular coordination, is used to produce the highest strength increases and inhibition of the central nervous system (CNS). The maximal-effort method allows for the recruitment of the maximal number of motor units and optimal discharge frequencies, together with key biomechanical parameters. This method maximally stimulates the Type II fibers, especially the high force-output fibers. However, it does not fully stimulate all fibers, and thus does not maximally stimulate muscle hypertrophy.

Repetition ranges are between one and three for structural power lifts (e.g., cleans, snatches), for which the aim is maximal power. For exercises that aim to develop strength (e.g., squats), repetition ranges are between two and six.

This type of training should only be used by experienced athletes who have sound technique. Even when training experienced lifters, care needs to be taken in the application of this method, as it is a highly intense form of exercise that places a great deal of stress on the CNS, and which if continued for excessive duration can result in an overtraining syndrome.

Repeated-Effort Method

In this system, a lighter load is used and a higher number of repetitions are performed to failure. In addition, a submaximal system can be employed in which the exercise is ceased before failure is reached. Both systems are effective for the production of hypertrophy, with the repeated-effort method slightly more productive than the submaximal method. However, if the athlete is training for strength, the set needs to be taken to failure, as only then will the maximal number of motor units be recruited and fatigued—a requirement for strength development.

Dynamic-Effort Method

In the dynamic-effort method, the aim is to develop the rate of force production and explosive strength via the use of lighter weights and high movement speeds. Methods can include throwing implements, medicine balls, and ballistic-resistance exercises.

Choosing the Resistance

In the programs outlined in this book, repetition ranges are utilized rather than poundages or percentages of 1 RM. Thus, 8–10 RM refers to a weight that will incur momentary muscular failure within the repetition range given. This type of programming requires the selection of a weight that initially allows performance at the lower end of the range (i.e., 8). Over the next few workouts, the aim would be to increase the repetitions achieved with this weight to the upper range (i.e., 10). At that point, the weight would be increased by an amount that allows for the performance of the lower repetition figure. This process is then repeated throughout the training period. In general, strength and explosive-power workouts employ lower repetitions (three to five), while muscle hypertrophy is best achieved with higher repetitions (8 to 12).

Exercise Order

Multijoint exercises, stressing the largest musculature, require a greater energy input and thus are placed early in a workout. Explosive exercises require maximal power output, and are thus compromised by any fatigue. With these issues in mind, athletes should always adhere to the following exercise order:

- Explosive exercises
- Multijoint lower-body strength exercises
- Multijoint upper-body strength exercises
- Isolation exercises, if required

Occasionally (but rarely), this order will be overridden when a specific program aim is emphasized. For example, an athlete whose main goal is to develop upper-body strength may perform the bench press early in the workout to allow for full effort during this exercise.

Training Frequency

At least two sessions per week need to be performed for each key movement to develop strength and hypertrophy. While one session per week can maintain strength for a period, two are generally needed to achieve gains. Three workouts per body part are generally appropriate in the off-season, with two being more common in-season, considering the increased game and practice commitments.

Whole-Body Versus Split Routines

In the initial stages of training, whole-body routines are recommended. Whole-body routines train all of the key movements and exercises in one session. However, when large numbers of exercises are performed or when loadings are high, it is recommended that split routines be introduced, with each session stressing different exercises and strength factors.

A multitude of different split routines can be employed. A two-day split breaks the workout into two sessions, each of which is normally repeated twice weekly. A three-day split normally breaks the workout aspects into three parts, to be performed on three consecutive days and then repeated after a day of rest.

Sample Two-Day Split Systems

Upper-body/lower-body—In this type of program, the athlete performs all of the lower-body exercises on one day and then returns either later in the day or the next day to perform the upper-body workout.

Strength/explosive—In this type of program, the athlete performs all of the explosive exercises on one day and then returns the next day to perform the strength exercises. This system can also be used for training two sessions in one day.

Sample Three-Day Split Systems

Explosive heavy/strength/explosive light—In this type of program, the athlete would perform a heavy day of explosive lifts on day 1. This workout would be followed by a strength workout on day 2 and a light explosive workout on day 3.

Explosive/lower-body/upper-body—In this type of program, the athlete performs all of his explosive lifts on the first day, all of his upper-body exercises on the next day, and then returns the next day to perform the lower-body workout.

Light and Heavy Sessions

Lifting at consistently high intensities of 1 RM can result in high levels of fatigue. Therefore, it is important to schedule heavy and light sessions. In heavy sessions, high loads are lifted, resulting in high levels of neural fatigue. The next session can be light, normally utilizing approximately 10 percent less resistance than the heavy session. Moderate sessions, when used, normally use 5 percent less load than heavy sessions.

Recording Strength Sessions

Recording performance is a vital part of any program and should include details of the exercises performed, the sets completed, the loads, and the repetitions. Recording allows for quantification of the training load and creates a clear record of progress that can also ascertain where an athlete stands at any time.

Periodizing Strength Training

Research has consistently proven that periodized training is superior to training that does not have a structural pattern of development. Clearly, the nature of the periodized program will depend upon the specific requirements of a given sport. Within a yearly cycle of preparation, the following phases are normally seen:

The hypertrophy phase—The repeated-effort method is used during this stage, with repetitions in the 6-to-12 range. Shorter rest periods are utilized, which stimulate the anabolic hormones and condition muscles prior to the increased intensity of exercise in the following phases.

The strength phase—The repeated-effort method is increasingly replaced at this stage by the maximal-effort method. Loads are increased and repetition ranges drop to two to six. Rest between sets increases to allow for maximal effort on subsequent sets.

The power phase—This stage represents the precompetition period, when the goal is to peak the power output of the athlete. The maximal-effort method is dominant, utilizing Olympic lifts as well as key structural exercises. The repetition range is low (i.e., two to five) and rest between sets high. In addition, the dynamic-effort method is utilized with a range of resistances that depend on the exercise.

Warming Up Prior to Strength Sessions

Warming up must involve raising the core temperature, mobilizing key muscles, and performing movements that will be included in the workout, but at a lower intensity. The workout preparation covered in Chapter 4 is also ideal for strength sessions. Following the workout-preparation program, a number of light progressive-resistance sets (normally one to three, depending on the exercise) of the exercise to be performed are completed, with the resistance increasing with each set in preparation for the first working set. These sets do not count as working sets.

Bodyweight Exercises

These exercises provide an excellent introduction to resistance training. They can also provide an alternative for when the athlete does not have access to a weight room.

Free Body Squats (Figure 7-1)

Objective: To development good squat technique without loading the spine and joints

Description: Stand with your feet parallel and toes pointing slightly outward. The heels should be slightly wider than the hips. Keeping the feet flat on the floor, flex at the hips and descend until the upper thighs are parallel to the floor.

Figure 7-1

Coaching Points:

- The knees should stay in line with the ankles and should never move beyond the toes.
- The back should remain in a neutral position, at the same angle as the shins.
- The body weight should be on the whole foot, not forward on the ball of the foot.
- The eyes should look forward at all times.
- The chest should be pushed forward and up.

Single-Leg Squats (Figure 7-2)

Objective: To progress from the two-legged squat, while also adding a stability factor to the exercise

Description: Squat on one leg as low as possible without losing balance or control, thereby reaching "the balance position."

Coaching Points:

- Proper alignment of the leg is crucial in this exercise.
- Adhere to the coaching points for the Free Body Squat.

Figure 7-2

Hamstring Lowers (Figures 7-3 and 7-4)

Objective: To develop both eccentric and concentric strength in the hamstrings, but also emphasize movement at the hip rather than at the knee. This exercise is therefore more movement-specific to soccer than knee-based exercises such as leg curls.

Description: Kneel on the edge of a stable exercise bench with your feet protruding over the edge. Have a partner secure your feet firmly against the bench. Keeping the body straight, lower the body forward as far as possible, and then raise the body back to the starting position.

Coaching Points:

- The body must remain straight. No flexion can occur in the lower spine.
- Progression occurs via lowering the body further forward.
- Further progression can be provided by holding weights.

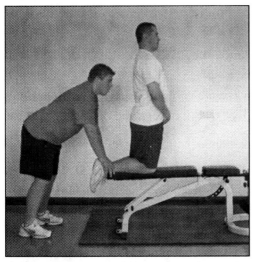

Figure 7-3

Figure 7-4

Medicine-Ball Lunges (Figure 7-5)

Objective: To build strength and stability in the quadriceps and glutes, and build core strength in the torso

Description: Stand with a medicine ball held overhead and with your feet parallel and hip-width apart. Take a step forward and lower the front leg until the shin reaches a 90-degree angle to the floor and the thigh is parallel to the floor. Push down with the front leg and take a step back to the starting position. Repeat with the other leg for the desired number of repetitions.

Figure 7-5

Push-Ups

Objective: To build basic strength in the major "pushing" muscles—pectoralis, deltoids, and triceps—and develop general torso stability

Description: Choose the appropriate exercise from the following progression. The aim is to choose an exercise that allows for between six to 12 repetitions. Assume the start position, ensuring the body is held in a straight-line "neutral" position.

Progression:

• Basic push-up (Figure 7-6)

• Offset push-up (one hand is forward and the other is back) (Figure 7-7)

- Medicine-ball push-up (one hand is placed on the medicine ball and the other on the floor) (Figure 7-8)

- Two-hand medicine-ball push-up (two hands are placed on the medicine ball) (Figure 7-9)

- Explosive roll (one hand is placed on the medicine ball and you explosively perform the push-up by simultaneously rolling the ball to the other hand and landing in the starting position, but with the ball in the other hand) (Figure 7-10).

Figure 7-6

Figure 7-7

Figure 7-8

Figure 7-9

Figure 7-10

Coaching Points:

- At no time should any extension or flexion occur in the lumbar spine or at the hips.
- These exercises (with the exception of the explosive roll) should be performed in a slow, controlled manner.
- The shoulder blades should never protrude out from the back.

Note: A number of progressions are outlined for this exercise. Athletes should choose the most advanced progression that allows for the completion of the recommended repetitions.

Chin-Ups (Figures 7-11 and 7-12)

Objective: To develop basic strength in the major "pulling" muscles of the upper back and biceps

Description: Assume an overhand wide grip. Hang from a chin-up bar, ensuring full extension of the arms. Slowly pull the body up so that the chin rests over the bar. Slowly lower to the starting position.

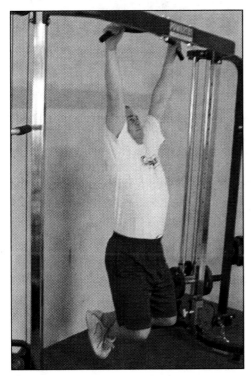

Figure 7-11

Figure 7-12

Push-Up Twists (Figures 7-13 and 7-14)

Objective: To develop stability against rotary forces and strength in the obliques and lower back

Description: Assume a push-up position. Raise one hand from the ground and simultaneously twist the torso so that it finishes at a 90-degree angle to the floor.

Progression: This exercise can be performed with one hand on a medicine ball.

Figure 7-13

Figure 7-14

Glute Leg Raise/Bird Dog

Objective: To develop strength and firing patterns in the gluteus maximus and stability in the pelvic girdle

Description: Assume a four-point position with the knees on the floor and the thighs perpendicular to the floor. Keeping the hips square and a stable knee angle, raise the right leg so that the thigh reaches a position parallel to the floor. Hold this position for a two-second count, lower, and repeat. Repeat on the opposite leg.

Progression:

- Simultaneously raise the opposite arm as the leg rises (Figure 7-15).
- For more difficulty and more rotational forces, raise the same-side arm (i.e., right arm, right leg).

Coaching Points:

- The hips must remain square and should not tilt laterally.
- Movement should be slow and controlled.

Figure 7-15

Resistance Exercises

Squat (Figures 7-16 and 7-17)

Objectives: To develop excellent strength in the quadriceps, gluteus maximus, hamstrings, and thigh adductors; develop strength in the ligaments surrounding the knee; and develop stabilization strength in the torso

Starting Position:

- Place the bar on the rack at chest level.
- Place your hands on the bar slightly wider than shoulder-width apart in an overgrasp grip.
- Step under the bar, keeping the feet parallel and bending the knees slightly.
- Rest the bar on the trapezius above the posterior deltoids.
- Keeping the torso straight, squeeze the shoulder blades together. The chest should be up and out.
- Extend the knees to lift the bar off the rack.
- Step backward and place the feet parallel, slightly wider than the hips, and with the toes pointing slightly out.

Movement: Focus your eyes straight ahead and maintain this focus throughout the exercise. Inhale deeply, bend at the hips and knees, and descend slowly and with control, until the upper thighs are parallel to the floor. Maintain knee alignment with the feet, and do not allow the knees to extend past the feet. Keep your body weight on the whole foot and keep your back straight. Start to exhale as you rise out of the "hole." Continue to rise until your knees and hips are fully extended.

Note: It is recommended that the squat be performed in a power rack, which allows for the setting of pins so that the weight can be "caught" if an attempt is failed or the lifter loses control.

Figure 7-16   Figure 7-17

Dead Lift (Figures 7-18 through 7-20)

Objective: To strengthen key extensor muscles and low-back musculature

Description: Address the bar with the bar over the middle of the shoelaces when you are looking down. Descend to grasp the bar by moving as if you are sitting into a chair. The hips should move backward as you descend. Grasp the bar with an over/under grip. Lift your head and look ahead or up. Dip the hips. Push up with the legs while the upper body maintains its alignment. Then, thrust the hips forward to straighten the body. Finally, reverse the movement to lower the bar, moving the hips backward, and then bend the knees to place the bar back on the floor.

Coaching Points:

- The back should be neutral throughout the exercise, with the head in line or slightly extended.

- The eyes should be focused straight ahead or slightly upward throughout the exercise.

- The chest should be held up and out with the shoulder blades squeezed together.

- The bar should remain as close to the body as possible throughout the exercise.

- In the initial movement, no extension should take place in the back. Instead, the exerciser should simply perform a leg-press movement.

Figure 7-18

Figure 7-19

Figure 7-20

Single-Leg Split Squat (Figure 7-21)

Objective: To develop unilateral leg strength

Description: Place a bench directly behind you and grasp two dumbbells. Place one foot on the bench and the other foot forward. Lower the hips into a parallel squat position. Return to the starting position.

Figure 7-21

Step-Up (Figures 7-22 through 7-24)

Objective: To develop unilateral strength

Description: Set up a box of appropriate height in a power rack. The box should be between midshin and knee height. Hold two dumbbells and stand approximately one foot away from the box with your feet parallel. Hold the body as you would for a squat, with the chest out and forward and the scapulae pulled toward each other. Take a step onto the box with the lead leg, placing the whole foot firmly on the box. Shift the weight onto the front foot, with the back foot still in the start position. Forcefully extend the lead hip and knee, stepping the trail leg onto the box (do not bounce or push with the trail leg). Shift your weight onto the lead leg and step down with the trail leg. When the trail leg is on the floor, shift the weight to this leg and step down with the lead leg. Start the next repetition by stepping up with the opposite leg first.

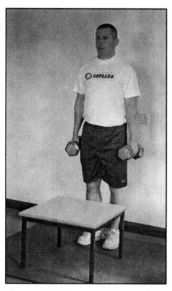  

Figure 7-22   Figure 7-23   Figure 7-24

Lunge (Figures 7-25 and 7-26)

Objective: To develop unilateral strength in the key leg and hip-extensor muscles

Description: Stand with two dumbbells held at arm's length. Take a large step directly forward until the shin of the lead leg is at a 90-degree angle to the floor. Lower the trail leg until the knee is approximately an inch above the ground. The thigh of the lead leg should be parallel to the floor. Keep the knee directly over the front foot. Balance the body weight between the whole of the lead foot and the ball of the trail foot. Keep the torso upright. Press the front leg into the floor and push back to the start with one movement, rather than with stutter steps.

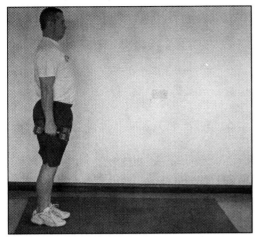

Figure 7-25

Figure 7-26

Coaching Point:

• This exercise can be performed by completing a set number of repetitions on one leg before switching legs, or by alternating the lead leg on each rep.

Leg Press (Figures 7-27 and 7-28)

Objective: To develop strength and hypertrophy in the quadriceps and gluteus muscles. This exercise is regarded as a secondary exercise to the squat.

Description: Sit in a leg-press machine and place your feet high on the footplate. Press the weight up and unlock the pin. Flex at the hips and knees and start the descent. Lower the weight until a 90-degree angle is attained at the knee. Press the weight back to the start by extending at the knees and hips.

Figure 7-27

Figure 7-28

Coaching Point:

• Do not allow the athlete to arch his back away from the backrest or lift his buttocks off of the seat.

Side Lunge (Figures 7-29 and 7-30)

Objective: To develop lateral movement strength

Description: Assume a standing position with dumbbells held at arm's length. Take a step sideways and lower the body weight toward the working leg until a 90-degree angle is achieved at the knee. Simultaneously take the dumbbells to the working leg. Press up to the start position.

Figure 7-29   Figure 7-30

Coaching Point:

• This exercise can be performed by completing a set number of repetitions on one leg before switching legs, or by alternating the lead leg on each rep.

Calf Raise (Figures 7-31 and 7-32)

Objective: To develop strength in the plantarflexors and ankle joints

Description: Assume a position with your shoulders under the pads of the calf machine. While maintaining a straight posture, extend the knees. Plantarflex the foot as high as possible. Slowly lower to a point of stretch and then repeat the movement.

Figure 7-31   Figure 7-32

Romanian Dead Lift (Figures 7-33 and 7-34)

Objective: To develop strength in the hamstrings and lower back

Description: Grip the bar in an overhand grip, with your hands slightly wider than shoulder-width apart. Stand upright with your feet shoulder-width apart and pointed straight ahead. Unlock the knees and bend forward so that the buttocks move backward. While maintaining a neutral spine, continue to bend until the bar reaches the midshin, or the hips cannot go back any further. Thrust your hips forward and raise your body to the starting position.

Figure 7-33   Figure 7-34

Glute Ham Raise (Figures 7-35 and 7-36)

Objective: To develop strength in the gluteus, hamstring, and calf complexes

Description: Position yourself in the machine so that the midthigh is on the pads and the feet are supported. Slowly lower the upper body by flexing at the hips. At the conclusion of the descent, extend the hips to come up to a position where the body forms a straight line.

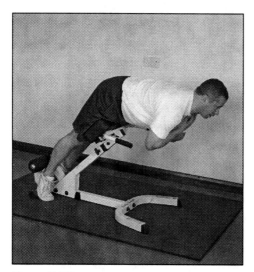
Figure 7-35

Figure 7-36

Coaching Point:

• Movement in this exercise occurs at the hips, not in the lumbar spine as in a back extension.

Note: This exercise requires a special bench or modified back-extension machine.

Bench Press (Figures 7-37 and 7-38)

Objective: To develop strength in the pectorals, deltoids, and triceps musculature

Description: Assume a prone position on a stable bench, with your feet flat on the floor. Grasp the bar with your hands slightly wider than shoulder-width apart, and simultaneously squeeze your shoulder blades inward and push your chest outward. Press the bar off the racks with the bar over the chest. Inhale and slowly lower the bar to touch the chest at approximately nipple level. Press the bar back to the start position. The feet should remain firmly on the floor.

Figure 7-37   Figure 7-38

Incline Dumbbell Press (Figures 7-39 and 7-40)

Objective: To develop strength in the pectorals, deltoids, and triceps musculature

Description: Set the bench to a 30-degree incline. Assume a strong position with the feet firmly on the ground. Have a spotter lift the dumbbells to your chest. Press the weights to arm's length, which is the start position for this exercise. Inhale and draw the shoulder blades inward and push the chest outward. Lower the dumbbells to touch the chest, and then press the dumbbells to arm's length.

Note: This exercise can also provide additional stabilization requirements to the barbell bench press and help alleviate bilateral deficits.

Figure 7-39   Figure 7-40

Bent Row (Figures 7-41 and 7-42)

Objective: To develop strength in the key "pulling" muscles: latissimus dorsi, trapezius, teres major, rhomboids, and biceps

Description: After lifting the bar, assume a position with the knees slightly bent and the back neutral and close to parallel to the floor. The bar will hang at arm's length. Pull the bar into the upper abdominals.

Figure 7-41

Figure 7-42

Seated Row (Figures 7-43 and 7-44)

Objective: To develop strength in the key "pulling" muscles: latissimus dorsi, trapezius, teres major, rhomboids, and biceps

Description: Assume a seated position with the feet against a footplate. Grasp the handles with a closed pronated grip. Keep the back erect. Pull the handles toward your chest, maintaining an erect torso position. While keeping the elbows next to the ribs, allow the handles to move back to the start position.

Figure 7-43

Figure 7-44

Pull-Down (Figures 7-45 and 7-46)

Objective: To develop strength in the key "pulling" muscles: latissimus dorsi, trapezius, teres major, rhomboids, and biceps

Description: Grasp the bar with a pronated grip with the hands wider than shoulder-width apart. Place your legs firmly under the pads and your feet on the floor. The arms should be fully extended at the start position Lean back slightly and pull the bar down toward the upper chest, finishing at a point near the clavicles. Lower the weight with control back to the start position.

Figure 7-45   Figure 7-46

Coaching Point:

•   Alternate grips or bars can be used with this exercise to provide variety (e.g., parallel grip, underhand grip).

Shoulder Press (Figures 7-47 and 7-48)

Objective: To develop strength in the shoulder musculature

Description: Set the bar in the racks at shoulder level. Grip the bar with your hands slightly wider than shoulder-width apart. Rest the bar on the upper chest. Press the bar overhead by extending the arms.

Note: This exercise can also be performed in a seated position.

Figure 7-47

Figure 7-48

Upright Row (Figures 7-49 and 7-50)

Objective: To develop strength in the deltoids and trapezius muscles

Description: Assume an overhand shoulder-width grip. Hold the bar at arm's length, with the bar touching the thighs. Flex at the elbows and pull the bar to the chin.

Figure 7-49

Figure 7-50

Coaching Points:

- Keep the bar as close to the body as possible.
- Keep the elbows pointed up throughout the movement.
- Keep the body upright with no forward lean.
- This exercise is sometimes used as a development exercise for pulling movements.

Rotational Exercises

Many traditional strength programs only use exercises that work in the sagittal plane. However, soccer is a multiplanar sport, and, therefore, rotational exercises need to be included in the programs.

Cable Lift (Figures 7-51 and 7-52)

Objective: To provide a stable trunk and hip base while producing rotational movements

Description: Attach a rope to a low pulley. Stand with your feet slightly wider than shoulder-width apart. Rotate the shoulders toward the pulley and grasp the handles with both hands. Keep the chest up and the core braced. Rotate away from the machine, initially pulling the rope to the chest. Continue the smooth movement by pressing the rope to arm's length and continuing to rotate. At the end of the movement, the back should be turned to the machine. Reverse the motion, lowering the weight to

Figure 7-51

Figure 7-52

the start position. The back should remain neutral (i.e., no flexion or extension). Continue for the required number of repetitions and repeat to the other side.

Note: This exercise can be performed in a kneeling position or while sitting on a stability ball. These alternatives add variety to the workout.

Cable Chop (Figures 7-53 and 7-54)

Objective: To provide a stable trunk and hip base while producing rotational movements

Description: Attach a rope to a high pulley. Kneel with the knee furthest away from the pulley on the floor. Rotate the shoulders and grasp the handles with both hands. With a smooth movement, rotate away from the pulley and pull the handles to the chest. Continue the movement and push the rope down and away. Be sure to rotate toward, and then away from, the machine as the movement progresses. The back must remain neutral, with the shoulder blades down. Continue for the required number of repetitions and repeat on the other side.

Note: This exercise can be performed while sitting on a stability ball or standing. These alternatives add variety to the program.

Figure 7-53   Figure 7-54

Cable Pulls (Figures 7-55 and 7-56)

Objective: To develop pulling strength

Description: Stand with feet parallel. Alternate pulling each handle from a low starting position into the chest. This exercise can also be performed in a staggered stance.

Coaching Points:

- Single-arm pulls can be used as an alternative.
- A single-leg stance can be assumed as a development for balance.

Figure 7-55

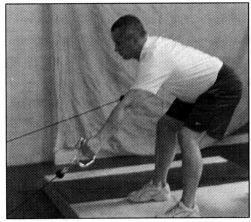

Figure 7-56

Explosive Exercises

Rack/Hang Clean (Figures 7-57 through 7-60)

Objective: To develop high rates of force development via triple extension of the hip, knee, and ankle musculature

Description: For the rack clean, set the bar in the power rack at a level just below the kneecaps. Grasp the bar with a clean grip. For the hang clean, dead lift the bar, and then lower it down to a position just below the kneecaps (i.e., the same position as for the rack clean). Assume a stance so that the shoulders are in front of the bar and the knees are slightly bent. Initiate the movement by extending the hips, which will have the effect of straightening the legs. The shoulders should lift straight upward. As the bar reaches above the knee, move the hips forward and re-bend the knees, bringing them down and in front of the bar. At this point, try to jump explosively upward, simultaneously rising onto the balls of the feet, straightening the body, and shrugging the shoulders as high as possible. As the shrug is complete, pull the bar as high as possible, as in an upright row. At the top of the pull, quickly dip to catch the bar. Rotate the elbows down and then up ahead of the bar. Catch the bar on the front of the shoulders. Flex the knees and hips to absorb the weight of the bar.

Figure 7-57

Figure 7-58

Figure 7-59

Figure 7-60

Clean

Objective: To develops explosive power in the key extensor muscles

Description:

*   Address the bar (Figure 7-61)
    *   ✓ Address the bar, with the bar over the middle of the shoelaces as you look down.
    *   ✓ Descend to grasp the bar by moving as if sitting into a chair. The hips should move back at this time.

Figure 7-61

- ✓ Grasp the bar with an overhand grip.
- ✓ The chest should be up and out and the shoulder blades should be pulled together. The head should be in line with the body or slightly extended.
- ✓ Lift the head and look up.
- ✓ The back should be neutral or slightly extended.
- ✓ Dip the hips.

- First pull (Figure 7-62)
  - ✓ Push up with the legs and lift the bar up and back. The upper body should maintain its alignment.
  - ✓ Your body weight should be on your heels.
  - ✓ The legs should be almost straight.

- Double-knee bend (Figure 7-63)
  - ✓ As the bar reaches above the knee, move the hips forward, and re-bend the knees, bringing them down and in front of the bar.

Figure 7-62

Figure 7-63

- Second pull (Figure 7-64)
  - ✓ Explosively extend the hips and knees, straightening the body as if trying to vertical jump with the bar.
  - ✓ Rise onto the balls of the feet, straightening the body and then shrugging the shoulders as high as possible.
  - ✓ As the shrug is complete, pull the bar as high as possible, as in an upright row.

- The catch (Figure 7-65)
  - ✓ At the top of the pull, quickly dip to catch the bar.
  - ✓ Rotate the arms around and then under the bar.
  - ✓ Catch the bar on the front of the shoulders.
  - ✓ Flex the knees and hips to absorb the weight of the bar.

Figure 7-64　　　　　　　　Figure 7-65

The Snatch

Objective: To develop explosive power in the key extensor muscles

Description:

- Address the bar (Figure 7-66)
  - ✓ Address the bar, with the bar directly over the middle of the laces as you look down.
  - ✓ Descend to grasp the bar by moving as if sitting into a chair. The hips should move back at this time.
  - ✓ Grasp the bar with a wide pronated grip.
  - ✓ The chest should be up and out and shoulder blades should be pulled together. The head should be in line with the body or slightly extended.

Figure 7-66

✓ Lift the head and look up.

✓ The back should be neutral or slightly extended, with the shoulders in front of the bar.

✓ Dip the hips.

- First pull (Figure 7-67)

✓ Push up with the legs and lift the bar up and back. The upper body should maintain its alignment.

✓ Your body weight should be on the heels.

✓ The arms should be straight, with the elbows out and wrists flexed.

✓ The legs should be almost straight at the end of the first pull.

- Double-knee bend (Figure 7-68)

✓ At the end of the first pull, move the hips forward and re-bend the knees, bringing them down and in front of the bar.

Figure 7-67

Figure 7-68

- Second pull (Figure 7-69)

✓ Explosively extend the hips and knees, straightening the body as if trying to vertical jump with the bar.

✓ Rise onto the balls of the feet, straightening the body and then shrugging the shoulders as high as possible.

✓ The arms should be straight, with the elbows out and wrists flexed.

✓ As the shrug is complete, pull the bar as high as possible.

- The catch (Figure 7-70)
    - ✓ At the top of the pull, quickly dip to catch the bar.
    - ✓ Rotate the arms around and then under the bar, pushing upward with the arms.
    - ✓ Jump the feet out into a wide squat stance.
    - ✓ Catch the bar overhead.
    - ✓ Flex the knees and hips to absorb the weight of the bar.

Note: The snatch can also be performed from a rack or hang position, as for the hang clean.

Figure 7-69

Figure 7-70

Power Press (Figures 7-71 through 7-73)

Objective: To develop explosive force in total-body extension and force transference from the lower body to the upper body

Description: Set the bar in the racks at shoulder level. Grip the bar with the hands slightly wider than shoulder-width apart. Rest the bar on the upper chest, with the chest pushed forward and up. Dip the legs, and then explosively extend the hips and extend the arms to lift the bar overhead.

Figure 7-71

Figure 7-72

Figure 7-73

Split Jerk (Figures 7-74 through 7-76)

Objective: To develop explosive force in total-body extension and force transference from the lower body to the upper body

Description: Set the bar in the racks at shoulder level. Grip the bar with the hands slightly wider than shoulder-width apart. Rest the bar on the upper chest, with the chest held forward and out. Dip the legs, and then explosively extend the hips and extend the arms to lift the bar overhead. While pushing against the bar, split the legs with one going forward and the other back. Immediately lower the body to catch the bar. To recover, take a step back with the front foot and then a step forward with the back foot to reassume the start position.

Figure 7-74

Figure 7-75

Figure 7-76

8

Power Training

Power can be thought of as strength at speed. Technically, it is defined by the following formula:

Power = force x distance/time

Power lies at the very essence of soccer performance, in which forces need to be applied rapidly. In the majority of cases in soccer, the time simply isn't available to exert maximal force. The ability to exert forces at speed is therefore more important. Power is dependent upon both maximal force and the rate of force production. A power-development program must focus on developing both of these aspects, as having one without the other greatly reduces a player's effectiveness.

The program presented in this chapter uses three key methods of developing power:

- Resistance training
- Plyometric training
- Medicine-ball training

The Power Pyramid

Initially, basic strength development in itself can develop power. Therefore, power-training methods should not be fully employed until a firm base of strength is developed. Thus, no power-based training is carried out with athletes in the base phase, as the body is not yet suitably conditioned to withstand this type of exercise. In the development stage, both plyometric exercises and explosive resistance exercises are introduced, but the initial emphasis is on the development of technique. Following this technical work, the athlete is able to introduce power exercises into the later phases, safe in the knowledge that the body has been prepared for this type of exercise.

Explosive Resistance Exercises

This program revolves around the use of Olympic-based lifting motions and their derivatives. These exercises are outlined in Chapter 7 and play a key role in the programs outlined in Chapter 14. Olympic lifts and their derivatives are an excellent method of developing highly specific power. They involve the key explosive triple-extension action, which is crucial for running and jumping. Technique is a crucial factor in the effective use of the Olympic lifts, and athletes should always develop sound technique before adding loads. Unlike strength-based exercises, the aim of the Olympic lifts is to achieve high power outputs, and repetitions are always kept low (one to three) to accommodate this goal.

In addition, other exercises are performed in an explosive way (e.g., the squat using the compensatory-acceleration method, where the aim is to move the bar as quickly as possible through the concentric part of the exercise). These methods and specific guidelines for the use of power-based resistance training are covered in Chapter 7.

Defining Plyometrics

Plyometrics are jump-based exercises that revolve around two key models, which together represent the stretch–shorten cycle. Taken together, these models have the capability of greatly increasing force production in a short period of time.

- The first model is the mechanical model. As a muscle is stretched, elastic energy in the muculo-tendinous units is increased and stored, which, if used immediately, can contribute to the subsequent concentric activity. The series elastic components of the tendons are primarily is responsible for this effect. This energy can only be effectively used if the concentric action immediately follows the eccentric action.

- The second model is the neurophysiological model, which is facilitated by the stretch reflex. As a muscle is stretched, stretch receptors in the muscle sense the rate and magnitude of stretch and elicit a contraction response to attempt to counteract the stretch. This action can add to the subsequent concentric force if little delay occurs between the stretch and the subsequent action.

To facilitate these effects, plyometric exercises require as short a pause as possible between the prestretch and the subsequent concentric action. Thus, a short ground-contact time should be stressed in all plyometric exercises

Categories of Plyometric Exercise

Plyometrics can be classified into two main categories:

- *Short response* (Figure 8-1)—Ground-contact time is exceedingly short with little displacement of the body.
- *Long response* (Figure 8-2)—Ground-contact time is a little longer, and a greater degree of displacement occurs.

Figure 8-1

Figure 8-2

Landing Technique

Proper landing technique is vital to ensure safe performance of plyometrics. When landing, the legs initially should be extended, with the feet in the dorsiflexed position. Foot contact should be on the balls of the feet, with an immediate bending of the knees to cushion the landing. The foot contact should then continue onto the whole foot, but with the overall weight slightly forward onto the balls of the feet. Good knee and ankle alignment should be maintained at all times. Figure 8-3 shows a sound landing position.

Figure 8-3

The Plyometric Pyramid

Plyometrics should be introduced after a base of strength has been developed. Also, they should be introduced progressively via a development program, the key aim of which is to develop landing technique and the ability to absorb eccentric forces and stabilize body positions. A suitable landing surface should be selected at all times. The surface should be soft enough to absorb some impact forces, but not too soft so as to reduce takeoff forces. Surfaces such as grass or sprung wooden floors are suitable for plyometric exercises.

The following progressions are used within the development program:

- *Jump up to box* (Figures 8-4 and 8-5)—When executing plyometrics, the greatest forces occur at landing and are generated by the athlete's bodyweight, accelerated by gravity. By jumping up to a box, the effects of gravitational acceleration are minimized, and therefore landing technique can be developed while landing forces are minimized, Jumping up to a box is an ideal way to develop the ability to land. When appropriate , intensity can be increased by increasing the height of the box or moving from double-leg to single-leg landings.

- *Jump and stick* (Figures 8-6 and 8-7)—Take a short jump and then freeze the landing position. Again, good landing technique and alignment need to be stressed. Intensity can be gradually increased by increasing the height or length of the jump or moving from double-leg to single-leg landings.

Figure 8-4

Figure 8-5

Figure 8-6

Figure 8-7

- *Short-response jumps* (Figure 8-8)—Take a series of short response jumps. Rapid foot contacts on the balls of the feet are key. In addition, it is essential that movement and body control are maintained throughout the exercise, as these aspects are the fundamental goals of this type of movement.

Figure 8-8

Plyometric Training

Once technique has been established and the athlete has been prepared for plyometrics via the development program, then the athlete can undertake a full plyometric program. Once good technique is established, maximum effort jumps will be used with a greater dependence on long-response drills (short-response drills are predominantly used as warm-ups). Plyometric drills used in this phase should emphasize vertical, horizontal, and lateral drills.

Foot contacts, or the number of times the feet hit the ground during a session, are a simple way of measuring plyometric volume. For example, five sets of depth jumps with four repetitions in each set provide a total of 20 foot contacts. As a guideline, the number of foot contacts within a session will vary between 60 and 200, depending upon the exercise intensity and the player's weight, stage of development, cycle of training, and playing commitments. The plyometric program can be completed within the main running session or within the explosive power-resistance workouts. Programs should incorporate movements that work vertically, horizontally, and laterally, and utilize both single- and double-leg takeoffs and landings as appropriate.

Types of Jumps

- *In-place jumps* (Figures 8-9 and 8-10)—In-place jumps involve single or repeated jumps that start and land in the same place.

Figure 8-9   Figure 8-10

- *Standing jumps* (Figures 8-11 and 8-12)—Standing jumps involve a single maximum effort. Examples include the standing broad jump and single box jump.
- *Multiple jumps* (Figures 8-13 and 8-14)—Multiple jumps involve a series of jumps that can emphasize vertical, horizontal, or lateral movement or a combination of the three.

Figure 8-11

Figure 8-12

Figure 8-13

Figure 8-14

- *Depth jumps* (Figures 8-15 and 8-16)—Depth jumps involve stepping off of a set height, landing, and immediately performing a jump.

Figure 8-15

Figure 8-16

Plyometric Intensity

It is important to control the intensity of plyometric exercises to ensure appropriate overload and progression. The intensity of the plyometric exercises will be determined by the following elements:

- *Speed of movement*—The greater the speed, the greater the intensity.
- *Points of contact*—Single-leg drills are more intense than double-leg drills.
- *Height/distance of jump*—The greater the height or distance of a plyometric jump, the greater the ground forces and thus the greater the intensity of the exercise.
- *Athlete weight*—Heavy athletes have to absorb greater forces than lighter athletes, which should influence the volume of foot contacts within a session and in the overall program.

Medicine-Ball Training

Medicine balls are ideal tools for multiplanar power development. Unlike resistance exercises that require a degree of deceleration prior to the completion of the exercises, medicine balls allow for acceleration through the entire range of movement and a subsequent release. Similarly, they allow for the development of rotational forces, which are important for soccer performance. Therefore, medicine balls are ideal for developing highly functional power.

It is important to remember the aim of a particular exercise, usually the enhancement of power. Repetitions are low within sets, allowing for maximum effort on all repetitions. Ideally, a range of medicine balls is utilized, as optimal weights exist for each athlete and each exercise. Because power is a product of force and velocity (velocity = distance divided by time), athletes should not compromise the velocity of each throw simply to enable themselves to use a heavier ball. Peak power output is essential.

Contrast training is a very effective way of enhancing power. A lighter ball is used after a heavy ball, providing a stimulus to the neuromuscular system. Contrast training can easily be integrated into medicine ball–based power sessions. In this method, a set of six medicine-ball throws may be set up as follows:

- Throw 1: 3 kg
- Throw 2: 3 kg
- Throw 3: 2 kg
- Throw 4: 2 kg
- Throw 5: 3 kg
- Throw 6: 2 kg

Medicine-Ball Exercises

Medicine-ball exercises can be included in resistance-training sessions or general conditioning sessions. They provide an ideal method to enhance multiplanar power. Maximum effort must be stressed at all times.

Overhead Throw (Figure 8-17)

- Hold a medicine ball overhead in two hands.
- Plant one foot and throw the ball as far as possible, utilizing a prestretch.
- Alternate the planted foot with each repetition.

Side Throw (Figure 8-18)

- Hold a medicine ball in two hands.
- Assume a stance at a 90-degree angle to where you want the ball to go.
- Use a prestretch and rotate the body away from the direction of movement.
- Immediately throw the ball as hard as possible.
- Throw in both a forehand and backhand direction.
- The throw can be performed on one leg to add a balance dimension.

Figure 8-17   Figure 8-18

Front Rotational Throw (Figure 8-19)

- Hold a medicine ball in two hands.
- Stand facing directly to where you want the ball to go.
- Use a prestretch by rotating the body away from the direction of movement.
- Immediately following the prestretch, throw the ball as hard as possible.
- Throw in both a forehand and backhand direction.
- The throw can be performed on one leg to add a balance dimension.

Backward Rotational Throw (Figure 8-20)

- Hold a medicine ball in two hands.
- Stand facing in the opposite direction of where you want the ball to go.
- Use a prestretch by rotating the body away from the direction of movement
- Immediately following the prestretch, throw the ball as hard as possible.
- Throw in both a forehand and backhand direction.
- The throw can be performed on one leg to add a balance dimension. However, this variation will reduce the total power output.

Figure 8-19

Figure 8-20

Forward Throw for Height (Figures 8-21 and 8-22)

- Assume a loaded position.
- Use a prestretch. Immediately after, throw the ball as high as possible.

- Actively jump as the ball is released.

Note: A variation to this exercise is a forward throw for distance.

Figure 8-21

Figure 8-22

Backward Throw for Height (Figures 8-23 and 8-24)

- Assume a loaded position.
- Use a prestretch and throw the ball as high as possible back over your head.
- Actively jump as the ball is released.

Note: A variation to this exercise is a backward throw for distance

Figure 8-23

Figure 8-24

Chest Pass (Figure 8-25)

- Hold a medicine ball in two hands.

- Plant one foot forward and perform a powerful chest pass.

- Alternate the lead foot with each repetition

Woodchop (Figure 8-26)

- Hold the medicine ball overhead to one side.

- Using a prestretch, throw the ball to the ground to the opposite side.

Figure 8-25   Figure 8-26

Constructing the Medicine-Ball Workout

Medicine-ball training can be carried out as a separate session or incorporated into the strength session. Exercises can be supersetted with resistance exercises to both provide a contrast and exploit the potentiation effects of heavy resistance training. When selecting exercises, ensure that each of the following throw types are incorporated into the work:

- Triple-extension-based exercises (e.g., forward throw for distance)

- Rotation-based exercises (e.g., front rotational throw)

- High-to-low-based exercises (e.g., woodchops)

Note: Many of the medicine ball exercise can be performed on one leg. This variation adds a dynamic balance element to the exercise, but reduces peak power output. When deciding whether to use a one-legged exercise, it is important to determine the main aim of the exercise.

9

Core Training

A key feature of soccer is the need to transfer force from the primary lower-body force producers to the upper body and upper extremities. This transfer occurs during such activities as heading and shooting. Force transference requires a stable base, which is provided by a strong torso. Therefore, core strength and stabilization is essential to high-quality soccer performance, and is an essential part of a soccer conditioning program.

To ensure effective core-stability training, it is vital to follow a progressive plan. The exercises presented in this chapter, which are presented in increasing levels of difficulty, represent only a small sample of those available. It is important that progression through the exercises is based upon successful completion of the previous stages of exercises. Technique must never be compromised.

The Nature of Core Stability

Core stability refers to the degree of body control over the lumbar, pelvic, and hip complexes. Effective force transference requires a stable base. Therefore, increased stability in this core musculature can enhance movement efficiency and effectiveness and aid in injury prevention by providing optimal alignment of body segments. An important principle to apply to any conditioning program is the need to develop stability before strength or power.

A look at soccer movements clearly illustrates the importance of the core musculature. With increased core stability and strength, the athlete is provided with a firmer "base" around which to perform, which in turn facilitates:

- The ability to exert greater power outputs in soccer-specific environments
- More effective force transference between body segments
- Less compensatory movements in other body segments, resulting in more efficient movement
- Improved dynamic balance, allowing for effective force transference in optimal alignment
- Improved posture
- Decreased injury risk through improved alignment of body segments. Proper alignment results in a more effective recruitment of appropriate movement patterns and a reduced need for compensatory actions to correct muscle imbalances or improper muscle recruitment.

The Principles of the Pyramid Approach

As with all fitness parameters, an effective method of sequencing and progressing core training to allow for optimal development is vital. Although many athletes may already utilize the exercises presented in this chapter, along with many other exercises, many simply perform the exercises without considering the underlying aim of each exercise. While some results will come with this approach, progress is less then optimal. As with any exercise program, a sound base is essential, and, as with any skill-development program, optimal results will only manifest when fundamental skills are mastered. The approach outlined in this chapter provides a sound progressive program, which starts with fundamentals and then progressively moves to more advanced exercises, while always developing and enhancing the fundamental skills. This program effectively applies the key training principle of progression. Work at the higher levels is based upon mastery of the basic skills, thus optimizing the results to be gained from the advanced exercises.

When looking at each exercise, an athlete must focus on the aim of each level. Failure to do so will compromise results. Although exercises at the initial levels may look easy, especially to individuals with extensive athletic backgrounds, they are fundamental to the success of the program and it is imperative that an athlete not move on to more advanced exercise until the basic-level work has been mastered. The fundamental aim of each level is as follows:

Base—Mastery of core contraction, postural alignment, and static holds in a stable environment

Development—Static holds in an unstable environment and dynamic movements in a stable environment

Peak—Dynamic movement in a stable and unstable environment

Muscle Actions

To fully understand the principles of core-stability training, it is important to first have an understanding of the basic anatomy of the core, as well as the key roles and functions of each muscle. In simple terms, muscles can be looked at as falling into two categories, mobilizers and stabilizers. Superficial muscles, such as the pectoralis group and quadriceps group, are generally mobilizers, meaning that their main function is to produce movement. Each movement has its prime mover, or agonist muscle, along with the corresponding antagonist muscle, which is able to slow down or stop the movement. For example, in a biceps curl the biceps are the agonist and the triceps are the antagonist. Traditional resistance-training techniques can effectively develop mobilizing muscles.

Another group of muscles exists that also plays a key role in sports performance, but which receives far less emphasis during traditional resistance-training programs. These often deep muscles play a stabilizing role. Stabilizers play a key role in sports performance because mobilizing muscles can only function optimally on a stable base, regardless of their strength. Despite this key role, stabilizers are not stressed during many training protocols. Core-strength training attempts to directly target these stabilizing muscles.

Developing Core Strength

Core strength, as with the majority of other fitness variables covered in this book, is best addressed through an appropriate development program. This program takes a pyramid approach, starting with the base phase, developing through to the peak phase. Each phase has its own specific aims, and each successive phase is based upon the successful completion of the previous phase.

The Base Phase

The base phase develops the basic fundamentals of core stability. This phase predominantly involves developing the ability to contract key core muscles and to maintain neutral alignment in a stable environment. Progression is brought about by increasing the duration of each hold.

This phase requires the athletes to master the contraction of the core muscles and understand and master the principles of pelvic control. Athletes at this level are required to actively contract the core muscles and hold these contractions, and to achieve a neutral spine and pelvis via an effective brace position. The aim then is to progressively challenge the ability to hold the static contractions and maintain pelvic and lumbar control. The exercises generally require athletes to move into and hold static positions. The aim of all of these exercises is to maintain stability and control positions via muscular contractions of the core muscles.

Base Exercises

The Basic Transverse Contraction (Figure 9-1)

Objective: To isolate the transverse abdominis and learn to contract the muscle voluntarily, leading into a full brace position

Description: Place your thumbs on your navel and extend the fingers toward the pubic bone. Draw the navel gently away from the thumbs by contracting the transverse abdominis muscle. Then, gently contract all of the muscles of the abdomen and low back to produce a corset effect. The navel should return to the thumbs. The brace should generally be a gentle contraction rather than a maximal contraction, as a gentle contraction can be held for a long period of time.

Coaching Points:

- Breathing should continue as normal.

- The athlete should feel the contraction with the fingers.

- The athlete should experience a feeling is as if he is trying to get into a tight pair of jeans while contracting the transverse abdominis.

- The athlete should hold the contraction for increasing durations.

- Practice is the key, as this brace motion is fundamental to many of the movements at subsequent levels.

Variations:

Figure 9-1

- Placing a biofeedback monitor between the abdomen and a belt can give a visual indication of the contraction.

- The contraction can be performed supine, using a puck or similar object as a visual cue.

- A rope drawn tightly around the waist can act as a visual cue to master the brace motion.

- The athlete can carry out the contraction and brace at cue points during the day (e.g., every time a class bell rings).

The Reverse Ramp (Figure 9-2)

Objective: To utilize leg and hip musculature while maintaining a neutral position

Description: Lie supine in a crook position (i.e., knees flexed to 90 degrees, heels on the ground, and toes raised). Brace the abdominals, tighten the gluteals, and raise the hips off the ground to form a straight line from shoulders to hips. Hold the position.

Figure 9-2

Coaching Points:

- The athlete should maintain the braced position.
- The athlete should hold a neutral lumbar position.
- The athlete must hold the position for the required duration.

Variations:

- Holding a foam roller between the knees will increase the activation of the pelvic floor muscles.
- This exercise can be performed with a single leg, which will increase the difficulty and add a rotary stress, thereby developing stability in the transverse plane.

The Plank (Figure 9-3)

Objective: To maintain core stability in a stable environment while maintaining neutral spinal alignment

Description: Place the forearms on the floor under the shoulders and lower the body into a push-up start position while maintaining a neutral spine. Brace and hold the position for the required time.

Figure 9-3

Progressions:

• Perform the exercise with your eyes closed.

• A coach can add pressure to the body to test the stable position.

• Progress to a full push-up position.

• Progress to a one-arm position.

Coaching Points:

• The athlete must achieve a neutral spine.

• The athlete should maintain the braced position throughout the exercise.

• The athlete should keep the scapulae drawn down and retracted.

Side Bridge (Figure 9-4)

Objective: To develop control of the oblique muscles and quadratus lumborum on a stable base

Description: Assume a side-lying position. Straighten your legs and cross the upper leg in front of the lower leg. Keeping the shoulders square, lengthen the body, and then brace and push the body up to a straight-line position supported by the forearm of the lower arm.

Figure 9-4

Coaching Points:

- The pelvis and shoulders must remain square, with the whole body in a straight line from head to toe.
- The athlete should maintain the braced position throughout the exercise.

Four-Point Pelvic Shift (Figures 9-5 and 9-6)

Objective: To maintain stability while unloading the limbs

Description: Assume a four-point kneeling position. Slowly shift the weight onto one leg, and then lift the opposite leg a maximum of two inches off the ground while maintaining a straight line across the pelvis. Repeat with the other leg. Aim to ensure that the stick stays in place.

Figure 9-5

Figure 9-6

Coaching Points:

- This is a key exercise to master prior to performing leg-raising activities.
- The braced position must be maintained throughout the exercise.

- The hips must remain square with no pelvic rotation.
- The stick should remain in a straight line.

Note: In the initial stages of learning this exercise, place a stick across the upper pelvis to indicate neutral position. Doing so provides an ideal visual indicator to enhance learning. This step can then be dispensed with once proper positions can be identified and maintained.

Development Phase

Once the athlete is able to master the concept of the neutral spine and maintain this position in stable environments, unstable environments can be introduced to add progression to the program. The aim is to progressively challenge the ability to maintain the alignment of the pelvis and spine via holding of the core contractions. The use of the unstable environment is fundamental to the progressive challenge to the core-control positions. Progressive practices are set up in which athletes are asked to statically hold progressively more challenging positions or to produce movement in stable positions. All of the exercises in the development and peak programs can be progressed by:

- Increasing the duration of holds
- Increasing the number of repetitions
- Making a smaller base of support (e.g., by placing the feet closer together)
- Reducing the points of contact (e.g., single-leg)
- Closing the eyes
- Adding resistance (e.g., medicine balls, partner pressure)

The Bridge (Figure 9-7)

Objective: To maintain stability in an increasingly unstable environment

Description: Sit on a stability ball. Walk out to a point where the shoulders remain on the ball and the legs are flexed to 90 degrees. Brace and hold the position as steady as possible for the required time.

Progressions:

- Perform the exercise with your eyes closed.
- Raise your hands until they touch together (reducing the base of support).
- Hold the foam roller between your knees (to help activate the pelvic floor).

Figure 9-7

- Raise one foot off the ground.
- Extend the leg to a straight-out position.
- A coach can add pressure to the body to test the stable position.

Coaching Points:

- The braced position should be held at all times.
- The athlete should avoid excessively utilizing the erector muscles to maintain the position.
- The athlete should ensure that the body is held in a straight alignment and doesn't extend or flex.

The Reverse Bridge (Figure 9-8)

Objective: To maintain neutral spine and core stability in an unstable environment

Description: Move into a push-up position with two feet on the ball. Brace and hold a position that is as stable as possible.

Figure 9-8

Progressions:

- Place your hands a greater distance from the ball.
- Decrease the distance between the hands.
- Perform the exercise with your eyes closed.
- A coach can add pressure to the body to test the stable position.
- The coach can tap on the ball to test stability.
- Raise one leg off the ball.
- Place your hands on a medicine ball.
- Use single-arm support.

Coaching Points:

- Neutral position of the spine must be maintained.
- The braced position must be maintained throughout the exercise.

The Side Bridge (Figure 9-9)

Objective: To develop strength in the oblique muscles and stability against rotational force

Description: Place an elbow and forearm on a balance mat and extend the body laterally away from the floor. Press the elbow and forearm into the mat and simultaneously use the obliques to raise the body off the floor to a straight-line position.

Coaching Points:

- The braced position must be maintained throughout the exercise.
- The athlete must maintain a straight-line alignment of the body.

Figure 9-9

The Ramp (Figure 9-10)

Objective: To maintain core stability in an unstable environment, and to enable the body to counteract perturbations (rapid shaking movements) that are generated by this movement

Description: Place your hands directly on the ball and lower the body into a push-up start position while maintaining a neutral spine. Brace and hold the position for the required time.

Figure 9-10

Progressions:

- Perform the exercise with the eyes closed.
- A coach can add pressure to the body to test the stable position.
- A coach can tap on the ball to create additional instability and the need to adjust to external stimuli.

Coaching Points:

- The athlete must maintain a neutral spine.
- The braced position must be maintained throughout the exercise.

The Reverse Ramp (Figure 9-11)

Objective: To maintain stability in an increasingly unstable environment and while the hamstrings are contracting

Description: Lie supine on the floor, with the feet placed flat on a stability ball. Brace, tighten the glutes, and raise the hips so that the body is in a straight line from the shoulders to the knees.

Figure 9-11

Progressions:

- Perform the exercise with your eyes closed.
- Raise your hands until they touch together (reducing the base of support).
- Hold a foam roller between your knees.
- Lift one foot off the ball.
- Extend one leg to a straight-out position.
- A coach can add pressure to the body to test the stable position.

Coaching Points:

- The braced position must be held at all times.
- The athlete should avoid excessively utilizing the erector spinae muscles to maintain the position.
- The athlete must ensure that the body is held in a straight alignment and doesn't extend or flex.

The Peak Phase—Adding Movement

The aim of the peak phase is again to provide a progressive challenge to the core contractions and the positions of stability and control. Progression involves the incorporation of movement into the unstable environment through exercises such as twists on the stability ball, together with dynamic movements in a stable environment. In addition, light resistance is added to some movements and an increasing amount of soccer-specific movements patterns and positions are assumed.

This phase is the culmination of the program, during which work becomes highly specific and dynamic—the essence of sports performance. This type of work provides a great challenge to the ability to hold core contractions and to hold positions of alignment and stability. Exercises done at this stage utilize methods of resistance such as medicine balls and resistance bands to add another more dynamic stimulus to the exercises and to make them more sport-specific. The added resistance allows for the development of very functional power, but at the same time maximizes core stability and control.

Crunches (Figure 9-12)

Objective: To develop strength and range of motion in the rectus abdominis

Description: Lie on a stability ball, with the ball in the small of your back. Brace and perform a crunch movement.

Progression:

- Add resistance in the form of medicine balls, resistance bands, or cable resistance.

Figure 9-12

Coaching Point:

- The athlete must maintain the braced position throughout the exercise.

Torso Twists (Figures 9-13 and 9-14)

Objective: To rotate at the waist against a stable pelvic area

Description: Assume a bridge position with a medicine ball held overhead. Brace, and while maintaining pelvic alignment, rotate as if to place the medicine ball on the floor to the side. The range of movement should be stopped when pelvic alignment is lost (i.e., when the pelvis dips laterally).

Progressions:

- First, increase the range of motion.
- Second, increase the resistance by using heavier medicine balls or dumbbells.

Coaching Points:

- The pelvis should be held square.
- The athlete should rotate to both sides.
- The braced position should be maintained throughout the exercise.

Figure 9-13   Figure 9-14

Reverse Bridge Pull-In (Figures 9-15 and 9-16)

Objective: To contract the rectus abdominis while maintaining pelvic control and core stability

Description: Assume the reverse bridge position. Brace, and while maintaining pelvic alignment, slowly draw the feet toward the hands as in a squat thrust exercise.

Figure 9-15   Figure 9-16

Coaching Points:

- This exercise must be performed slowly.
- The athlete must maintain pelvic control.
- Neutral back position must be maintained throughout the exercise.
- The athlete must maintain the braced position.

The Pike (Figures 9-17 and 9-18)

Objective: To strengthen the abdominal muscles while providing a challenge to core stability

Description: Assume a reverse bridge position. Brace, and while holding the legs straight, draw the feet toward the ball. The body will move into a pike position. Flexibility of the hamstrings will sometimes determine the finish position.

Figure 9-17

Figure 9-18

Coaching Points:

• The legs must be straight throughout the exercise.

• The athlete must maintain the braced position throughout the exercise.

• Movement occurs at the hips, not at the lower back.

North, South, East, West (Figures 9-19 and 9-20)

Objective: To achieve shoulder and core stabilization on an unstable base

Description: Assume a ramp position. Brace and then move the ball forward, backward, left, and right.

Figure 9-19

Figure 9-20

Progression:

• Increase the range of motion.

Coaching Points:

• The scapulae should remain depressed and should not bulge.

• Movement should be sufficient to provide stimulus, but not so much that it causes the athlete to lose form.

• The neutral position must be held at all times.

• The athlete must maintain the braced position throughout the exercise.

Ramp Elbow Crunches (Figures 9-21 and 9-22)

Objective: To perform abdominal crunches while maintaining the core contraction

Description: Assume a ramp position on the ball and then lower the body so that it is resting on the elbows, but with the scapulae elevated (i.e., stay high on the ball). Brace and perform a crunch movement by moving the elbows toward the waist.

Figure 9-21   Figure 9-22

Progression:

• Performing a prestretch, with the ball moved away from the body, greatly increases the intensity of the exercise.

Coaching Points:

• The braced position should be maintained throughout the exercise.

• The athlete must always stay high on the ball.

• Movement should only occur at the waist, meaning that the athlete must try to maintain pelvic stability throughout the exercise.

• The athlete must not allow the body to sag.

Log Rolls (Figures 9-23 and 9-24)

Objective: To develop rotational strength

Description: Assume a reverse bridge position, but with the thighs resting against the ball. Brace and rotate at the hips so that the thighs rotate 90 degree from the start position. Pause briefly and reverse the movement.

Figure 9-23

Figure 9-24

Coaching Point:

• The athlete must maintain the braced position and a neutral spinal alignment throughout the exercise.

Skiers (Figures 9-25 and 9-26)

Objective: To develop rotational strength

Description: Assume a reverse bridge position, but with the thighs resting against the ball. Brace and rotate at the hips so that the left leg comes over the right and rests gently on the ball on its medial side, while the right leg takes most of the weight on the lateral side. Pause briefly and reverse the movement.

Figure 9-25

Figure 9-26

Coaching Points:

- This exercise is a progression from the log roll.

- The athlete must maintain the braced position and a neutral spinal alignment throughout the exercise.

Medicine Ball Explosive Crunch (Figures 9-27, 9-28, and 9-29)

Objective: To withstand and immediately repel impact forces through the core

Description: Lie with your lower back resting on the ball and assume a finished-crunch position. Receive the ball from a coach with your arms outstretched, and then immediately throw it back to the coach, aiming for maximum power output.

Figure 9-27

Figure 9-28

Figure 9-29

Progressions:

- Increase the speed or distance of the throw.
- Increase the weight of the medicine ball.

Coaching Points:

- The athlete should keep the time between the catch and throw as short as possible to maximize the benefit of the stretch–shorten cycle.
- The athlete must maintain a stable base and pelvis.

Variation:

- Throws can be carried out in all directions.

Note: All of the medicine ball exercises demonstrated in Chapter 8 will develop effective core strength and can be integrated into the core program at this time.

10

Endurance Training

Soccer is played over a 90-minute period, with the ball in play for a large proportion of the time. The length and activity-level of the game emphasize the importance of being able to maintain the key attributes of speed, agility, power, and strength throughout the duration of the game. Endurance is therefore an important element of any soccer conditioning program. When designing a soccer endurance program, it is important to note that a large number of the key movements in soccer are performed at a high intensity, and that a period of recovery often exists between these high-intensity bouts of activity. Soccer performance does not involve continuous slow running. In this way, the key facets of the game are fueled both aerobically (with oxygen) and anaerobically (without oxygen), and both of the energy systems must be developed.

In soccer, the aerobic energy system generally is concerned with the replenishment of ATP and PCr and the removal of metabolite build-up (e.g., lactic acid and its associated build-up of H+), as well as fueling the lower-intensity movements during a game. The anaerobic system, on the other hand, fuels the higher-intensity activities such as sprinting, tackling, and heading.

To adhere to the rule of specificity, endurance work should replicate the requirements of the game, and should therefore be a series of high-intensity movements, interspersed with period of recovery (active or passive) , an interval training approach. With the importance of stressing both anaerobic and aerobic energy systems, it is essential that appropriate exercise intensities are elicited that allow the targeting of each energy system. When developing the endurance program, it is important that appropriate periods of rest are allocated between activity bouts to ensure that the intensity of exercise can remain high and the anaerobic energy system is adequately stressed. Similarly, work performed on exercise bikes and stairclimbers, for example, will not transfer well to soccer performance, and so the training program needs to revolve around running-based activities. This sport-specific training will allow the key local muscle adaptations to take place, in addition to the central adaptations (e.g., cardiovascular, respiratory). Whenever possible, movements similar to those found in the game should be stressed to allow the key muscle adaptations to occur in the muscles actually involved in a specific movement. Direction changes need to be incorporated, as do position-specific tasks such as jumping for headers.

Speed and Strength Reserve

A key feature of the endurance-training system outlined in this book is the emphasis on the speed and strength reserve, in addition to directly addressing the energy systems themselves.

Speed Reserve

The speed reserve refers to the difference between an athlete's peak speed and the levels required to perform during a game. If an athlete is able to run the 40-yard dash in 4.6 seconds and in a game is required to run the same distance in 5.3 seconds, then he has a speed reserve of 0.7 seconds, meaning that he is operating at a relatively low percentage of his top speed. In comparison, an athlete with a best time of 5.1 seconds, asked to cover the distance in 5.3, will only have a speed reserve of 0.2 seconds, meaning that he is operating at near-maximal levels. The second athlete clearly places a far greater load on the body, consumes more energy, and induces far greater fatigue.

To increase speed reserve, training programs should emphasize extensive use of speed training and speed-technique development, with a goal of making movement more efficient (refer to Chapter 5). These factors are essential to optimal endurance and can increase endurance without directly training the energy systems, as optimal endurance is not possible without these reserves.

Strength Reserve

The strength reserve refers to the difference between maximum force and the force required to carry out a game-related movement. For example, if an athlete has a large force capacity, a tackle will require a smaller percentage of that force capacity. The greater an athlete's maximal strength, the greater his strength reserve during any activity.

Strength-reserve training programs should develop high levels of strength and coordinated power (refer to Chapters 7 and 8). Increased strength ensures a high strength reserve and the fluid, coordinated exercise ensures energy-efficient movement. The weight room is used for strength and power development, not endurance, meaning that high-repetition sets are not generally recommended. Soccer strength requires the performance of relatively high-force activities, such as shooting and tackling, rather than the repeated performance of low-force activities. Therefore, endurance work is carried out in a soccer context and not in the weight room.

With all strength and speed programs, the aim is to increase maximum output, which will automatically increase work capacity and, in turn, endurance. This program design works on the principle that with a higher work output, submaximal tasks will represent a lower percentage of the new peak, thereby requiring lower energy input and creating a higher capacity for work.

Program Variables

Intensity—How hard a person works on each repetition, with full effort requiring 100-percent intensity. Intensity will determine which energy system is taxed, and it is vital that the appropriate intensity is selected to target the appropriate energy system.

Volume—The total amount of exercise carried out in a session. In general, the greater the volume, the lower the intensity. Where high intensities of work are required, the volume should be controlled to ensure appropriate energy-system development.

Recovery—The rest between repetitions. Anaerobic work tends to be done on a 1:3 to 1:5 work/rest ratio, with the higher the intensity, the higher the ratio. To facilitate quality performance, some sets can be divided to allow for greater recovery (e.g., 10 repetitions can be divided into two sets of five, with a 10-minute break between sets to allow for a greater intensity on each repetition, while still maintaining an appropriate volume).

Work duration—This factor depends upon the energy system to be taxed. ATP-PCr sessions will normally involve high-intensity work durations of four to eight seconds, while glycolytic sessions will normally involve high-intensity work lasting 20 to 90 seconds. Aerobic activities will be performed for one minute to 40 minutes, and the overall intensity will be lower than for anaerobic work.

Exercise type—Within a soccer program, the use of long, slow runs is limited to the occasional recovery session. Instead, the running program should attempt to replicate the types of activities found in soccer, with brief high-intensity efforts interspersed with periods of active recovery. Small-sided games are the preferred method of endurance training for the majority of the sessions outlined in this book.

Key Aspects of Performance

Analysis of the motion characteristics of soccer reveals that the following elements are key indicators of soccer endurance performance. These factors represent the key aspects of performance that need to be enhanced through training:

- ATP-PCr system development—Ensuring that this system if developed to allow the athlete to produce repeated high-quality runs
- Lactate tolerance—Ensuring that the athlete is able to tolerate any acidic build-up during a game, and that its effect on performance is minimized as much as possible
- Recovery from lactate build-up—To enable the body to clear lactic acid form the working muscles during a game, utilizing the aerobic system to facilitate this clearance
- Lactate threshold—The point at which lactic acid starts to accumulate in the working muscles. An increase in the lactate threshold is achieved by increasing aerobic power, so that a given work rate can be achieved via the aerobic system.
- $\dot{V}O_2max$ and velocity at $\dot{V}O_2max$—The maximum oxygen consumption an athlete can achieve, which is an indicator of overall aerobic power. This factor is dependent upon how the athlete is able to deliver oxygen to the working muscles (via the cardiovascular and respiratory systems), and utilize it for energy production at the working muscles. In addition to $\dot{V}O_2max$, the speed of running at which $\dot{V}O_2max$ is achieved is also important.
- Speed and strength reserve—The difference between the speed or strength required for the task and the maximal strength- or speed-performance levels.

Small-Sided Games

Traditionally, soccer endurance training has been carried out via running tasks, often involving extended distance running, which bears little resemblance to the requirements of the game. Increasingly, small-sided games are being viewed as a very viable alternative to this approach and have been proven successful in improving performance. Additionally, they are very time-efficient and can enhance athlete motivation by providing a very game-related task.

Small-sided games involve using traditional soccer games, but are played on a smaller playing area and with a reduced number of players. This format increases the number of actions a player has to perform in a given time. In this way, overload can be provided more so than in a normal game. In addition to a traditional game format, many of the games used to develop skills can be adapted for this purpose. All games can be modified to provide the appropriate level of intensity by adjusting the playing area, number of players, and game duration, and by feeding balls in (this is particularly effective in increasing intensity, as it eliminates down-time when a ball is out of play). By modifying the games, different intensity levels can be achieved as required for effective endurance training.

Once the game is set up, a sets-and-reps system can be utilized, just as with any interval-training technique. A sample session for a squad of 24 could be organized as follows:

- Play a small-sided soccer game, four versus four on a pitch 25 yards by 20 yards.
- Use a traditional pitch layout and rules, with the 24 players divided into six teams of four.
- Use a game duration of two minutes with continuous ball feeds.
- The first group of eight players (two teams of four) works for a two-minute game.
- At the conclusion of this game, the next eight players work for two minutes. At the conclusion of the second game, the remaining eight players work, after which the first eight players return for their second repetition. This process continues until all groups have completed six games. After a 10-minute rest the whole process is repeated.

This workout provides an interval session of two sets of six two-minute repetitions, with four minutes recovery between reps (1:2 work to rest ratio) and 10 minutes of rest between sets. However, unlike the traditional interval approach characterized by straight-line running, the movement patterns are soccer-specific and involve skilled actions.

Methods of Training the Aerobic System

To add precision to the aerobic training normally delivered by small-sided games, five zones can be identified as shown in Figure 10-1. The key to soccer conditioning is to maximize the aerobic benefit while minimizing any negative effects on other key fitness parameters such as strength, speed, and power. Therefore, the aim is to utilize the zones that give the greatest specific benefit while avoiding activities that provide the worst benefit/cost ratio. For soccer, training needs to be concentrated in zones 1, 4, and 5. The other zones are not intense enough to optimally affect $\dot{V}O_2$max, and eat into recovery ability and can negatively affect strength and power by altering fast-twitch fiber characteristics and neural firing.

Zone 1 Training

This zone involves relatively low-intensity training, with heart rates between 55 and 70 percent of maximum, but allows for development of the central aspects of aerobic

Zone	Goal	Intensity	Work-Bout Duration	Work/Rest Ratio
1	Aerobic base training	55–65% MHR	30–45 minutes	1:1 or continuous
2	Higher-intensity aerobic-base development	60–75% MHR	30–60 minutes	1:1 or continuous
3	Increased anaerobic threshold	75–80% MHR	5–10 minutes	1:1; 1:1.5
4	Improved lactate recovery	80–90% MHR	2–5 minutes	1:2
5	Increased $\dot{V}O_2max$, increased capacity at $\dot{V}O_2max$	>90% MHR	1–4 minutes	1:3
MHR = Maximum heart rate				

Figure 10-1. Systems of aerobic training

performance (i.e., cardiovascular and respiratory). It targets predominantly slow-twitch muscle fibers and therefore does not have the negative effects on fast-twitch fibers and neural input that are found in some of the higher zones. These types of sessions are used predominantly as recovery sessions after games or as light, recovery sessions within a periodized in-season program. Occasionally, they are used as introductory sessions for athletes with a poor aerobic capacity. Zone 1 training involves keeping the heart rate in the training zone for 30 to 40 minutes. Athletes need to avoid the temptation to raise the heart rate into other zones, as the session goal is to specifically enhance this zone of function. For soccer, running-based sessions should dominate this type of program. Alternatively, swimming can be used to facilitate recovery or be utilized if an athlete needs to reduce stress on joints.

Zone 4 Training

This training zone aims to develop a high anaerobic threshold and the ability to clear higher levels of lactic acid. For soccer, bursts of two to five minutes of activity are performed with rest periods in a 1:2 ratio. Small-sided games or running activities provide an ideal method of employing this type of activity. In a season's periodized program, zone 4 is used more extensively in the preseason, with zone 5 training dominating toward the end of the precompetition phase and during the competition phase.

Sample Session

The game outlined in the small-sided games section is an example of a level 4 game—a small-sided soccer game (e.g., four on four) with continuous ball feeds. Athletes can perform two minutes of activity and rest for four minutes between games, with active zone 1 rest being utilized. Two sets of six games are performed with 10 minutes of rest between sets.

Zone 5 Training

Zone 5 training involves intense bursts of activity lasting for 60 seconds to four minutes. This activity is then interspersed with active rest, in a ratio of approximately 1: 3, with the exact recovery time depending upon the actual intensity and duration of the work. Activities can involve running, small-sided games, or obstacle courses. The latter two of these activities help simulate the stop-start, multidirectional, repeated-sprint nature of soccer. Recovery between bouts should be active and in zone 1.

The use of sets and repetitions allows for a greater volume if high-intensity work is to be performed. For example, a series of 10 3-minute bouts of activity are better performed as two sets of five repetitions with a rest period of seven to 10 minutes between sets, rather than as one set of 10 repetitions. This design allows for a level of recovery that in turn allows for a higher intensity to be maintained throughout the runs.

Sample Session

Athletes can play two-on-two soccer in a 20-yard square area, with minigoals and no goalkeepers. Balls are fed continuously to reduce any down time, and goals can only be scored from within an area five yards from the goal. Athlete should perform 90 seconds of activity with four minutes of rest between repetitions.

Anaerobic Conditioning

Many key elements in soccer are anaerobic and, therefore, anaerobic conditioning is essential for optimal performance. Developing high levels of anaerobic capacity and power are the key aims of a soccer endurance program. Figure 10-2 gives guidelines on constructing anaerobic-based endurance sessions.

ATP-PCr System Development

The aim of training in this area is to enhance the capacity of the body to repeat short bursts of high-intensity activity via the ATP–PCr system. Work intensities are high and rest periods are long enough to ensure that intensity of effort remains high. Activities can involve running or soccer-specific movements (e.g., dribbling, tackling).

System	Goal	Intensity	Work-Bout Duration	Work/Rest Ratio
ATP-PCr	Enhance phosphate capacity	Maximum effort	5-8 seconds	1:4-1:25
Glycolytic	Enhance ability to produce energy under extreme acidosis	85%-plus of peak time	20-60 seconds	1:3-1:6

Figure 10-2. Anaerobic training

Sample Session

Athletes can perform two sets of five 60-yard sprints with 40 seconds of recovery between repetitions and 10 minutes of recovery between sets.

Glycolytic System

Work to enhance the glycolytic system is very intense, raising the athlete's capacity to tolerate high levels of lactic acid and facilitate its removal. Intensity can be gauged by utilizing percentages of the athletes' best time to cover a given distance. In this way, activities are normally performed at levels matching the maximum heart rate, and represent 85 percent-plus of an athlete's maximum speed over the distances run. These activities are interspersed with periods of active or passive rest in a ratio of 1:3–1:5, depending on the exercise intensity. The sets-and-repetitions method is used to ensure quality of effort, with up to 10 minutes of rest being recommended between sets. Total work volume is low (four to 12 repetitions), with no more than one session per week performed in-season and no more than two performed off-season.

Sample Session

Athletes can run 200 yards in a time 10 percent slower than their peak time. The athletes then walks back to the start in 2.5 minutes and repeat the run another four times. They then rest for 10 minutes, during which walking and light jogging take place. Repeat the entire sequence of sprints once more (for a total of 10 sprints).

11

Flexibility Training

Flexibility training is an important part of any conditioning process. However, unlike the other fitness variables covered, an optimum level of flexibility exists, above which performance will not improve. What is important is that an athlete has a sufficient level of flexibility to allow for smooth and efficient soccer movements.

The following sequence is designed to be used either as a postsession cool-down or more often as a separate regeneration session. Unlike many stretching routines that focus on stretches for individual muscle groups, this program aims to utilize movements that stretch multiple muscle groups and facilitate recovery. It blends a number of approaches, such as static stretching and yoga movements, into a functional session that addresses all of the key joints involved in soccer. This routine can also enhance relaxation and regeneration. The stretches outlined are designed to target a number of muscle groups, and will target areas in which an athlete requires additional flexibility. The same stretching movements will affect different athletes in different ways, targeting the specific weaknesses in each athlete's movement patterns.

When used as a separate regeneration session, the sequence should always be preceded by an activity to raise overall body temperature, such as jumping rope. The sequence provides a routine that moves logically from movement to movement and ends with more gentle movements to produce a relaxing effect.

When assuming the positions, athletes should use movements that are slow and controlled, along with deep and relaxed breathing. Similarly, when coming out of a position, movements should be slow and controlled and fluidly flow into the next position. Some of the movements may be challenging at first, but they will become more comfortable as a greater degree of flexibility is achieved. In general, the positions can be held for 20 to 30 seconds. Neutral alignment (as covered in Chapter 10) is important and should be stressed through the sequence. It is important to work for correct alignment, even if it initially results in a limited range of movement.

This routine is best performed on a soft surface, such as an exercise mat. Working outdoors on grass provides a suitable alternative.

Kneeling Position (Figure 11-1)

- Assume a kneeling position with the knees hip-width apart.
- The tops of the feet and toes should be flat on the floor with the toes facing away.
- Tuck in the tailbone and keep the back flat.
- The body weight should be back on the heels.
- Reach up and away with the arms, feeling a stretch through the upper body.

Camel (Figure 11-2)

- From the kneeling position, lift the thighs upward and forward to a position perpendicular to the floor.
- Tuck in the tailbone.
- At the same time, arch the upper body backward.
- Pull the scapulae down and attempt to reach back and push the arms to the floor.
- With high levels of flexibility, the hands will be able to cup the ankles.
- Return to the kneeling position.

Figure 11-1

Figure 11-2

Child's Pose 1 (Figure 11-3)

- From the kneeling position, reach the arms out in front.
- Bring the forehead down toward the floor.
- Simultaneously push the arms away.
- Relax and feel the stretch through the upper body.

The Pike (Figure 11-4)

- From child's pose 1, with the arms pushed away and palms flat on the floor, curl the toes under and press the tailbone upward into an inverted V.
- Push the heels toward the floor.
- Squeeze the elbows together to roll the scapulae down and out.

Figure 11-3   Figure 11-4

Upward-Facing Dog (Figure 11-5)

- From the pike, bring the hips down to the ground.
- Place the tops of the feet flat on the floor.
- Push the hands into the mat, scooping the chest and abdominals up.
- The thighs can remain on the floor or raised slightly.
- Pull the scapulae down, pushing the chest forward.
- Try to achieve a straight line between the shoulders, elbows, and wrists.

Child's Pose 2 (Figure 11-6)

- From upward-facing dog, reassume the kneeling position, but with the feet together and the knees pushed out to 45 degrees.

- Reach forward with the arms.
- Bring the forehead toward the ground.

Figure 11-5

Figure 11-6

Frog (Figure 11-7)

- From child's pose 2, bring the knees out as far as possible.
- Rotate the feet to face out and bring the shins parallel to the knees.
- The thighs and shins should be at right angles.
- Place the forearms flat on the floor, with the shoulders and elbows aligned.
- Raise the upper body and rest it on the forearms.
- Lower the hips back and down, pushing the knees out to the side.

The Pike (Figure 11-8)

- From the frog position, narrow the knees and assume the start position for the pike.

Figure 11-7

Figure 11-8

- Curl the toes under and press the tailbone upward into an inverted V.
- Push the heels toward the floor.
- Squeeze the elbows together to roll the scapulae down and out.

Warrior 1 (Right Leg) (Figure 11-9)

- From downward-facing dog, lunge the right foot forward between the hands.
- Rotate the back foot to 90 degrees and assume a long stance.
- Lower the front leg to 90 degrees.
- Reach the arms up and push away, simultaneously pushing the chest forward and up.
- The lower body should not rise.

Note: Repeat for the left leg.

Extended Side Angle (Right Leg) (Figure 11-10)

- From warrior 1, place the left hand flat on the floor.
- Raise the right arm straight up, creating a reaching feeling.
- Keep the tailbone tucked under and the chest forward.

Note: Repeat for the left leg.

Figure 11-9   Figure 11-10

Warrior 2 (Figure 11-11)

- Assume the same position as for warrior 1.
- Rotate the body so that the front arm is pointing straight along the front leg.
- The chest should be square and the scapulae should be pulled down.
- Push the arms away in opposite directions.

Note: Repeat for the left side.

Figure 11-11

Lunge Sequence (Figures 11-12, 11-13, 11-14)

- Assume a lunge position with the right leg forward and both feet facing forward.
- The body should be upright with the scapulae down and the chest forward and up.
- Push the arms upward (Figure 11-12).
- After 15 seconds, lean the body in the direction of the forward leg, but with no forward or backward lean (Figure 11-13).
- After 15 seconds, bring the upper body forward.
- Place the left hand outside the right leg and rotate the body. Hold for 15 seconds (Figure 11-14).

Note: Repeat for the left side.

Figure 11-12   Figure 11-13   Figure 11-14

Squat (Figure 11-15)

• From the lunge position, assume a full squat position.
• The feet should be hip-width apart, with the toes pointed ahead or slightly out and the heels flat.
• Aim to keep the upper body as upright as possible.
• Raise the arms overhead, pushing them backward.

Figure 11-15

Single-Leg Reach (Figure 11-16)

- From the squat position, drop into a crouched position with the right leg forward and the left tucked beneath the thigh.
- Hinging at the hip, reach the chest forward toward the knee.

Note: Repeat for the left leg.

Double-Leg Reach (Figure 11-17)

- Assume a seated position, with both legs extended.
- Again, hinge at the hip and reach the chest towards the knees.

Figure 11-16

Figure 11-17

Tabletop (Figure 11-18)

- From the double-leg reach seated position, bring the hands back approximately a foot behind the hips, with the palms flat and the fingers facing forward.
- Push to the floor and raise the hips.
- Drop the head back.

Supine Twist (Figure 11-19)

- From the tabletop position, return to a seated position and assume a supine position, with the arms extended straight out to the sides.
- Bend the right leg to 90 degrees.

- Grab the right knee with the left hand.
- Keeping the right arm on the ground, use the left hand to pull the right knee toward the floor on the left side of the body.

Note: Repeat for the left leg.

Figure 11-18

Figure 11-19

Reach (Figure 11-20)

- This exercise completes the routine and aims to elongate the spine.
- Stand with the feet together.
- Tuck the tailbone in.
- Reach to the sky with the arms straight and palms together.
- Tilt the head back, looking to the sky.
- Attempt to push down with the feet and up with the arms.
- Breathe deeply and relax the body.

Figure 11-20

12

Nutrition for Soccer

To achieve optimal results from the conditioning program, the athlete must combine it with quality nutritional intake. Sound nutrition plays a vital role in any conditioning program and is an essential part of the recovery process. It is important that the body is in an anabolic (i.e., muscle-building) state for as much time as possible and quality nutrition is a key element in achieving the anabolic state required for optimum performance gains. In an anabolic state, the body will respond to training by growing stronger and increasing its work capacity. However, if nutrition is poor, the body is likely to enter a catabolic, or breaking down, state in which performance gains will be compromised. Just as with physical training, a nutritional program needs to be well-planned. A sound soccer nutritional strategy must ensure that the diet provides the following:

- Sufficient carbohydrate-based calories to ensure effective refueling of energy stores
- Sufficient high-quality protein for tissue repair and muscle growth
- Sufficient minerals and vitamins for optimal body functioning
- An optimal level of hydration

Constructing a sound nutritional plan is a vital part of the overall conditioning program. The following guidelines provide a structure around which to base a high-quality nutritional program.

Add Color to Your Meals

As many meals as possible should include a liberal amount of fresh fruits and vegetables. This practice will ensure that a good supply of vitamins and minerals are included in the diet. It should also ensure that an adequate amount of fiber is incorporated into the nutritional program. Whenever possible, athletes should try to eat different colored fruits and vegetables, which is a simple way of optimizing the intake of all vitamins and minerals. Aim to have at least five servings of fruit and vegetables daily.

Eat Small Meals Frequently

Contrary to common beliefs and practices, the best way to eat is to consume five or six small meals per day, rather then the more common practice of eating a small number of very large meals. This routine helps to control blood sugar levels and also ensures regular supplies of nutrients to the body. This approach is best for both gaining lean body mass and losing body fat, with portion sizes determining whether the body will lose or gain weight. Frequent eating helps maintain the body's metabolism, assists in controlling body-fat levels, and ensures the body does not enter a period of catabolic activity brought about by lack of nutrients. Appropriate snacks and shakes are important tools in ensuring that food is consumed approximately every three hours.

Select Appropriate Protein Sources

Protein is a vital nutrient in the growth and repair of lean body tissue. A training program results in considerable muscle damage and the repair process is vital to the athlete. Regular supplies of protein are essential to the growth and repair process, and therefore to achieving the optimal results from a training program. Protein is best taken in via small, but regular, doses (as opposed to the usual approach of eating a large protein portion in two or three meals).

Protein is made up of different combinations of amino acids, of which two main types exist, essential and non-essential. Essential amino acids cannot be produced by the body, and therefore must be consumed in the diet. Non-essential amino acids, on the other hand, can be produced by the body. Therefore, it is important that the diet provides all of the essential amino acids. Complete proteins such as those found in animal products (e.g., meats, fish, milk, eggs) have all of the essential amino acids, and are therefore the preferred choice for protein. The essential amino acids are: valine, methionine, isoleucine, histidine, phenylalanine, thereonine, leucine, tryptophan, and lysine. When incomplete sources are used, they have to be combined to ensure that all of the essential amino acids are provided.

Athletes should aim to ingest at least 1 gram of protein per pound of body weight. The vast majority of this protein should be in the form of low-fat complete proteins such as fish, chicken, skim milk, and egg whites. In addition, protein can be taken in via shakes, which are especially useful as pre- and postworkout meals. Figure 12-1 provides guidelines for choosing proteins. For vegetarian athletes, appropriate food combinations of incomplete proteins that bring together grains and legumes must be consumed. Examples of such combinations include tortillas and beans, rice and beans, rice and lentils, rice and peas, and peanuts and wheat.

Best	Neutral	Worst
Skinless chicken	Chicken with skin	Fried chicken
95% lean ground beef	Turkey with skin	Heavily marbled beef
Fat-free milk	85–90% lean beef	Lamb
Nonfried fish or seafood	1–2% fat dairy products (milk, cottage cheese, yogurt)	Cheese
Skinless turkey	Whole eggs	
Tuna	Peanuts	
Egg whites	Trimmed pork chops	
Yogurt (low-fat, low-sugar)	85% lean ham	
	Lean turkey bacon	

Figure 12-1. Guidelines for choosing proteins

Choose the Right Type of Carbohydrates

Carbohydrates are the body's preferred source of fuel. The amount of carbohydrates ingested needs to be in relation to the activity level, and therefore needs to be higher on days of heavy activity and lower on less-active days.

However, not all carbohydrates are the same, and different types have a different effect on blood sugar. Some carbohydrates are rapidly digested and result in a rapid rise in blood sugar. The extent to which a carbohydrate causes a rise in blood sugar is termed its glycemic index, with foods high on the index causing a rapid release and those low on the index resulting in a slow, controlled release. Ideally, an athlete's carbohydrate intake should consist primarily of low or medium glycemic index foods. The consumption of high glycemic index foods should be limited, whenever possible, to postworkout meals, when a rapid rise in blood sugar is actually beneficial to replenishing the body's stores of carbohydrate in the form of glycogen. When high glycemic index foods are included in the meal, they should be eaten in small quantities and the majority of carbohydrate calories should come from low glycemic index foods. This plan helps reduce the glycemic load, which is calculated by multiplying the glycemic index by the number of calories of that food in the meal. Figure 12-2 lists the glycemic index of common carbohydrates.

In general, it is best to choose unprocessed, fresh produce. The more processing that is done to a food, the lower the nutritional value and often the higher the glycemic index. For example, whole-wheat bread is a far better choice than white bread.

Utilize Chrononutrition

Chrononutrition refers to the timing of meals. When people eat is just as important as what they eat. The need for small, regular meals has already been covered in this chapter, and chrononutrition is an extension of that rule. The key is to get the required nutrients into the body at the correct time and to reduce any periods of fasting.

Any chrononutrition program starts with breakfast, which must be viewed as the most important meal of the day. A good breakfast (like all meals) must consist of proteins and low glycemic index carbohydrates (including fiber). Following breakfast, food (or a shake) needs to be consumed approximately every three hours throughout the day. As the meals progress into the evening, carbohydrate intake should be reduced and protein intake should predominate. The last meal should be consumed shortly before bed and should include a lean protein source together with a nutrient-rich low glycemic index carbohydrate source.

Two important aspects of the chrononutrition program are the pre- and postworkout meals. Preworkout meals should provide energy for the forthcoming workout as well as protein that can be accessed for growth and repair immediately postworkout. Postworkout meals should replace used fuel stores and provide protein for muscle growth and repair. These two meals are absolutely essential for optimal training progress.

Immediately preworkout and during the workout itself, the athlete should attempt to take in nutrients, including carbohydrates, electrolytes, and protein. These nutrients provide energy in the form of glucose, but also have a glycogen-saving effect. The addition of protein reduces muscle breakdown and primes the body for the rebuilding process immediately following the workout. Consuming electrolytes helps replace those lost via sweating and is especially important in times of high heat and humidity. Maintaining hydration is also a key factor at this time. In the majority of cases, solid food will be either unavailable or inappropriate at these times. The consumption of sports

	Low Glycemic Index	Medium Glycemic Index	High Glycemic Index
Cereals	Regular oatmeal (not instant), All Bran™	Corn-based cereals, rice-based cereals, Shredded Wheat™	Sugar-coated varieties
Vegetables	Sweet potato, yams, asparagus, broccoli, sprouts, bell peppers, carrots, celery, mushrooms, tomatoes, cucumbers	Boiled potatoes	Parsnips, baked, and mashed potatoes
Fruit	Apples, apricots, bananas, cherries, kiwi, mangoes, oranges, blackberries, strawberries, raspberries, peaches, plums, blueberries	Dates	Sweetened fruit juices, canned fruits in syrup, melons, dried fruits
Breads and grains	100% stone-ground whole-wheat bread, whole-grain high-fiber bread	Whole-grain breads, pita bread	Bagels, baguettes, croissants, doughnuts, muffins, pancakes, white bread, granola bars, waffles
Rice and pasta	Basmati rice, brown rice, most types of whole-wheat pasta	Macaroni	White rice, instant rice, short-grain rice
Legumes	Baked beans (low-sugar), butterbeans, black-eyed peas, lentils, soy beans		Tapioca

Figure 12-2. Glycemic index of common carbohydrates

drinks is ideal for achieving the key nutritional aims. During games, halftime is an important time to refuel, and each athlete should ensure that appropriate refueling methods are available at this time.

The period immediately following training is the most important for the athlete. A window of opportunity exists in the first hour after a game or workout that peaks at 15 minutes and then reduces, finally closing an hour after activity ceases. If this key window of opportunity is missed, training gains will be compromised. It is essential that the body is primed to repair and rebuild muscle tissue, rehydrate, and replenish energy stores. Insulin is the key to achieving these goals. Insulin is a hormone stimulated by a rapid rise in blood sugar, and can act as an effective shuttle between blood sugar and the working tissues, carrying the required sugar to where it is needed for refueling. In this instance, high glycemic index foods are advised, as they rapidly break down and stimulate the secretion of insulin. In this way, the raw materials required for refueling are rapidly available at the muscles, enhancing the refueling process. Clearly

Timing	Type of Intake
Two hours preworkout	Eat low glycemic index carbohydrates (or a mixed meal with medium and low glycemic index carbohydrates) together with a moderate amount of protein. Drink 500 ml of water two hours before exercise.
Immediately preworkout, if needed (<20 minutes)	Eat or drink medium/high glycemic index carbohydrates with a small amount of protein (use a 4:1 ratio of carbohydrate to protein).
During the game or workout	Drink a medium/high glycemic index sports drink with a small amount of protein. Drink as much fluid as possible and replace electrolytes during longer sessions, or during sessions in high heat or humidity.
Immediately postworkout	Eat high glycemic index carbohydrates and a small amount of protein (use a 4:1 ratio of carbohydrate to protein; carbohydrate intake should be 1.5 g per kg of body weight).
Postexercise follow-up (as soon as possible after the game or workout)	Eat a meal with moderate/high glycemic index carbohydrates and mixed meals with protein

Figure 12-3. Guidelines for pre- and postworkout meals

postexercise nutrient intake is vital, and the athletes should ensure that they are able to take advantage of this process by having high glycemic index foods available immediately after training and games. Fluid intake is recommended at this time as well. Refer to Figure 12-3 for guidelines for pre- and postworkout meals.

Incorporate Good Fats

Fats often receive a great deal of bad publicity. The negative perception has resulted in the popularity of low-fat diets and the associated marketing of low-fat foods. It must be remembered that fats are an essential part of the diet and serve many functions that are required for optimum athletic performance.

A key point to remember is that all fats are not equal. Saturated fats (such as those found in animal-based products) and trans fat (as found in many processed foods) need to be limited, as these fats contribute to increased serum cholesterol levels. Unsaturated fats (especially fats such as olive oil, fish oil, flaxseed oil, and the fats found in nuts and seeds) should be included in the diet. The best and worst fat options are outlined in Figure 12-4.

Best	Neutral	Worst
Olive oil	Peanuts	Animal fats
Fish oil		Butter
Canola oil		Cream
Flaxseed oil		Whole milk
Sunflower seeds		Lard
Nuts (almonds, cashews pecans, walnuts)		Brazil nuts

Figure 12-4. Guidelines for fat intake

Drink Plenty of Water

A high level of hydration is essential for both optimal health and optimal performance. Just as with food, ingesting a little bit of water often throughout the day is the best plan. Ideally, an athlete would be sipping water all day and a water bottle would be seen as an essential part of the athlete's tool kit. It must be remembered that thirst is a poor indicator of hydration and that a thirsty athlete is already dehydrated. Urine color gives a good indicator of hydration level. Urine should be as pale as possible, as darker urine is a good indicator of an athlete close to, or in, a dehydrated state. In situations where a great deal of body fluid has been lost through sweating, add electrolyte-replacement drinks to the hydration strategy.

Follow the 1-2-3-4 Principle
When Planning a Meal

1. Select a range of fruit and vegetable sources.

2. Add a lean protein source, which should be no more than a quarter of the serving size.

3. Add low glycemic index carbohydrates, depending upon your energy expenditure (i.e., on hard training days the quantity consumed should be higher than on nontraining days).

4. Drink lots of water.

13

Recovery and Regeneration

Recovery is often the most overlooked aspect of a training program. According to the fitness fatigue theory (refer to Chapter 2), any training bout will result in an increase in fitness, but also a certain degree of fatigue, depending on the volume and intensity of the training, as well as a temporary drop in preparedness or performance level. Only after a period of recovery will preparedness rise, and recovery is therefore crucial to consistent gains in performance. Optimum performance and training progress depend upon a careful manipulation of the increase in fitness and the fatigue generated by the training as well as the use of recovery strategies to carefully manage these factors.

The Nature of Stressors

It has to be remembered that athletes are people, and soccer is only one part of their lives. At any time, they will be subject to a number of stressors, which exist in three main domains.

- Physical—Stress associated with training, competitions, and other physical tasks that are performed

- Psychological—Stress associated with psychological factors such as the pressure to perform and the pressure of examinations

- Emotional—Stress associated with feelings, beliefs, and relationships with others. Such stressors have the capacity to enhance or reduce overall energy levels.

Stressors are accumulative and can be thought of as collecting in a huge pot. At any time, the total stress on the athlete, and the response to this stress, will depend upon the combined effect of all stressors, together with the athlete's capacity to cope with the specific stressors. Although the stressors can be seen to exist in these domains, a cybernetic link exists between them, and it is the total stress on the athlete that is important—physical stress must not be viewed in isolation. This point is important, as the same training session may have a different overall effect, depending upon the athlete's ability to deal with the training stress. This ability in itself will depend upon the complex interrelationships among all of the things going on in an athlete's life and the ability to cope with these factors at any given time. It is important that the athlete and coach are aware of the overall levels of stress.

Multidimensional Recovery

Maximizing recovery needs to be an integral part of any training program. The athlete must ensure that recovery takes place in a multidimensional arena, meaning that it entails much more than physical rest. Given the complex nature of stress, an effective recovery and regeneration program needs to work on the following levels:

- Physical
- Psychological
- Emotional

Physical Recovery Strategies

Physical fatigue tends to occur in three main areas: physiological, neural, and tissue damage. Physiological fatigue relates predominantly to the energy systems, and recovery requires replenishment of these systems. Neural fatigue occurs in the mechanisms of the central and peripheral nervous systems, and recovery involves factors such as the replenishment of neurotransmitters. Tissue damage, as the name suggests, refers to fatigue caused by actual damage to tissues and is an issue in many physical contact sports, such as soccer. The following methods can be used to facilitate physical recovery:

- Nutritional strategies and the use of chrononutrition to maximise recovery after training and competitions (refer to Chapter 12)
- Hydrotherapy strategies
- Active recovery strategies

Hydrotherapy Strategies

Hydrotherapies can be very useful passive-recovery tools. A wide variety of hydrotherapies are available that can be employed at different stages of the recovery process to facilitate restoration of the athlete's performance. Whichever method is chosen, hydrotherapies should leave the athlete relaxed, but mentally alert. The duration of warm immersion should be controlled and should not result in lethargy.

Hydrotherapy in the form of ice baths or contrast showers can be used immediately post-training to aggressively enhance the recovery process. Figure 13-1 gives guidelines for the use of hydrotherapy strategies.

Pool recovery sessions can be used by individual athletes or groups of athletes to enhance regeneration. These sessions are best used either two or three hours post-training or, more commonly, on the morning following a game. Figure 13-2 shows an example of a pool recovery session.

Hydrotherapy Method	Guidelines
Contrast shower	• Use anytime. • Alternate one minute of hot (as hot as tolerable) with 30 seconds of cold. • Repeat three times.
Hot tub/ice plunge	• Use at the end of the training day. • Alternate two minutes in the hot tub (using the jets to massage key muscles and also stretching key muscles) with 30 seconds cold plunge (kneeling in waist-deep cold water). • Repeat three or four times. • Hydrate throughout the process by drinking water.

Figure 13-1. Hydrotherapy guidelines

Active Recovery Strategies

Periodizing the training program to include a variety of training loads and periods of active recovery is possibly the most important physical-recovery strategy. The periodization of training is extensively covered in Chapter 14 and is integrated into the overall program presented in this book. The concept of active recovery is important, as it involves a certain level of exertion rather than simply passive rest. This type of program helps promote the recovery mechanisms and also helps maintain performance levels during transition periods (refer to Chapter 14).

- Swim three lengths, one each of backstroke, breaststroke, and front crawl.
- Walk for three minutes in waist-high water, using a range of upper-body activities (e.g., sprint action, reaching up, side bends, rotations).
- Walk two widths, using full high-knee action, in shoulder-high water.
- Walk two faster widths, using high-knee running action, in shoulder-high water.
- Walk two widths, using an ankling action, in waist-high water.
- Swim two lengths, using the sidestroke (alternate sides).
- Walk two widths sideways, using a side-lunge action, in waist-high water.
- Swim three lengths, one each of backstroke, front crawl, and breaststroke.
- Walk two widths, crossover step–style, in waist-high water.
- Walk two widths, with a hip-circling action, in shoulder-high water (one length forward, one length backward).
- Walk two widths, lunging in waist-high water, with a variety of lunging combinations.
- Walk two widths backward, taking large steps, in waist-high water.
- Swim two lengths, using the sidestroke (alternate sides).
- Walk two widths, with a sprinter's paw-back action, in waist-high water.
- Walk two widths, with a high-kick action, in waist-high water.
- Jog two widths, in waist-high water.
- Spend five minutes statically stretching key muscles in the water.

Figure 13-2. Sample pool recovery session

In addition, the use of a stretching program (refer to Chapter 11) as either a postworkout cool-down or as a separate recovery session can enhance the entire recovery program. This program again promotes the body's recovery mechanisms and helps maintain the athlete's range of motion.

Psychological Strategies

Just as the body has a certain tolerance for physical training—and recovery periods are vital within any physical-training program—the same is true of psychological stress. The athlete cannot be psychologically active throughout the day without negatively affecting performance in the long-term. It is important that the athlete has access to methods that promote psychological recovery. Psychological strategies involve the ability to switch off from the stresses of the day and engage in activities that develop a feeling of relaxation and contentment.

It is important that an athlete develops interests outside of soccer, and that he is able to devote quality time to these interests. Additionally, the athlete should ensure that he is able to devote time each week to aspects of his life that he values, such as schoolwork and family. The ability to devote time to valued activities will assist in psychological recovery. The most appropriate strategies will be highly individualized, as what can relax one athlete may not work with another. What is important is the degree of control the athlete has over the activity. Watching a film, for example, will only be effective if the athlete is able to decide what film to watch and when. Being forced to watch someone else's choice will not be effective. The athlete needs to be in control of the strategies he chooses.

A major psychological barrier to performance is rumination, when problems go round and round in an athlete's head. Rumination has the potential to create massive psychological and emotional energy leaks, which can negatively impact recovery and performance. To help solve this problem, a disengagement strategy is key and should involve a performance debrief after any competition, during which the athlete writes down his feelings about his performance and sets actions plans for the next week's work. This simple process helps the athlete conceptualize his performance and helps reduce the need for rumination, as clear conclusions and plans are in place for the next few days. A similar daily debriefing, in which performance is evaluated and targets are set—both athletic and others—for the next day helps reduce the need for rumination.

Emotional Strategies

Remember, training stress must not be viewed in isolation. In reality, training is only one of a number of stressors within any athlete's life. Factors such as travel, work, relationships, and examinations all create stress. Stressors are additive and are related to the athlete's coping ability. To minimize stressors and maximize recovery, an athlete needs to enhance his emotional intelligence. Emotional intelligence involves an athlete developing awareness of his emotional performance, and then developing strategies to deal with any weaknesses, Emotional weaknesses can cause problems in an athlete's life that cause energy leaks, which subsequently reduce recovery. Developing emotional intelligence involves the development of awareness and strategies in two main domains, self- and social awareness.

Develop Self-Awareness

Athletes need to identify areas of their lives and performances that cause high levels of stress, as well their typical responses to these situations. This self-awareness is an important first step in developing an emotionally intelligent athlete. It allows athletes to become aware of their emotions and become more accepting of them. It also allows athletes to identify their reactions to emotions and their subsequent effect on performance, training, and recovery.

An important part of this process is examining the athlete's lifestyle and identifying potential sources of stress. These stressors may come from a range of sources, such as personal and team relationships. Figure 13-3 shows an effective way of identifying key lifestyle elements that may be contributing to stress levels. Once the major areas have been identified, strategies can be developed to help address any issues.

Once areas of concern are identified, strategies can be developed to either address issues or learn how to cope more effectively. These coping strategies are important, as they can stop potential sources of stress from developing. After developing these strategies, athletes will not be faced with so many potentially stressful situations, and athletes who can effectively cope will develop more optimism, which leads to a positive attitude and greater achievement.

An example of good self-management is an athlete who identifies an awareness of feelings of anger whenever performance does not go well, anger that continues into the evening. Left unattended, this issue could cause a long-term energy leak. Once the athlete is aware of the problem, he should look at the root cause of the anger, which could be a fear of what peers may say. A management strategy would then be to dispute the root cause of the anger, which is likely based on the athlete's belief rather that on concrete evidence. This strategy would then provide the basis for the management process, in which the athlete will focus on the support of his peers, removing the root cause of the anger and reducing its negative effects.

Develop Social Awareness

Soccer is a team sport. Therefore, the athlete will need to interact with players and coaches. All personal interactions have the capacity to either energize or de-energize an athlete, and an awareness of the impact of these interactions will help reduce overall stress levels and result in a much more effective level of functioning. Similarly, the need for social awareness will be equally as important in all aspects of the athlete's life, such as family, work, and school. By becoming aware of the effect his actions have on other people, the athlete is again able reduce the harmful effect of social stressors.

Developing an awareness of other people's perspectives and needs will assist in building effective personal relationships. This process builds upon the social awareness skill and helps the athlete interact with people in a way that reduces potential stressors. The athlete can then develop his ability to interact effectively with others. This practice will result in more effective conflict management, teamwork, and collaboration, all of which will contribute to a more efficient and stress-free work environment and lessen the emotional stressors on the athlete.

Lifestyle Profile

					The Scale						
I always get 8 hours sleep per night.	10	9	8	7	6	5	4	3	2	1	I never get 8 hours sleep per night.
My sleep is always of a good quality.	10	9	8	7	6	5	4	3	2	1	My sleep is never of a good quality.
I have a pattern of retiring and waking times.	10	9	8	7	6	5	4	3	2	1	I have no pattern of retiring and waking times.
I wake naturally each morning.	10	9	8	7	6	5	4	3	2	1	I never wake naturally in the morning.
I wake energized and motivated	10	9	8	7	6	5	4	3	2	1	I wake listless and demotivated.
I take in sufficient calories daily.	10	9	8	7	6	5	4	3	2	1	I do not take in sufficient calories daily.
I eat healthily at all times.	10	9	8	7	6	5	4	3	2	1	I never eat healthily.
I always eat breakfast.	10	9	8	7	6	5	4	3	2	1	I never eat breakfast.
I always refuel immediately after exercise.	10	9	8	7	6	5	4	3	2	1	I never refuel immediately after exercise.
I am able to manage my time effectively.	10	9	8	7	6	5	4	3	2	1	I cannot manage my time effectively.
I have no academic worries.	10	9	8	7	6	5	4	3	2	1	I have huge academic worries.
I have no financial worries.	10	9	8	7	6	5	4	3	2	1	I have many financial worries.
My other work schedules are realistic and in balance.	10	9	8	7	6	5	4	3	2	1	My other work schedules are unrealistic and out of balance.
I go to bed each night relaxed and unworried.	10	9	8	7	6	5	4	3	2	1	I go to bed each night stressed and worried.
I am able to find at least an hour's rest and relaxation time each day.	10	9	8	7	6	5	4	3	2	1	I am never able to find at least an hour's rest and relaxation time each day.
I have interests and activities that help me to relax.	10	9	8	7	6	5	4	3	2	1	I have no interests and activities that help me to relax.
I am in charge of me.	10	9	8	7	6	5	4	3	2	1	I have little control over my life.
Travelling commitments do not sap me of energy.	10	9	8	7	6	5	4	3	2	1	Travelling commitments sap me of energy.
I enjoy my sport.	10	9	8	7	6	5	4	3	2	1	I don't enjoy my sport.
My family life is relaxed and energizing.	10	9	8	7	6	5	4	3	2	1	My family life is stressful and de-energizing.
My social relationships are relaxed and energizing.	10	9	8	7	6	5	4	3	2	1	My social relationships are stressful and de-energizing.
My social life never impinges on my performance.	10	9	8	7	6	5	4	3	2	1	My social life always impinges on my performance.
I have great relationships with my teammates.	10	9	8	7	6	5	4	3	2	1	I have poor relationships with my teammates.
I have great relationships with my coaches.	10	9	8	7	6	5	4	3	2	1	I have poor relationships with my coaches.
I never drink alcohol.	10	9	8	7	6	5	4	3	2	1	I drink alcohol on most days.
My alcohol intake when I drink is minimal.	10	9	8	7	6	5	4	3	2	1	My alcohol intake on the days I drink is heavy.
I never smoke.	10	9	8	7	6	5	4	3	2	1	I smoke heavily.
I never take drugs.	10	9	8	7	6	5	4	3	2	1	I often take drugs.

Figure 13-3. Lifestyle profile

Sleep Strategies

Sleep is essential for optimal recovery and performance, and facilitates recovery in all three dimensions. Athletes should aim to get at least eight to nine hours of uninterrupted sleep per night. Quality sleep is as important as quantity. Sleep occurs in cycles lasting approximately 90 minutes. Initially, sleep is light, and only toward the middle of the sleep cycle do the deeper stages of sleep occur. It is during this deep sleep that the key physiological recovery processes occur. Deep sleep is important for physiological growth and repair. After deep sleep, the cycle continues as sleep gets lighter until a period of rapid eye movement (REM) sleep is reached. REM sleep is important for the restoration of neural functions. If sleep is disturbed, the whole sleep cycle will restart from the beginning. If such interruptions occur before deep sleep or REM sleep is achieved, it can negatively affect the number of deep and REM stages achieved within a period of sleep, thus reducing the restorative quality of the sleep. Figure 13-4 offers guidelines to enhance the quality of sleep. The earlier sleep cycles contain the greatest amount of deep sleep, while the later cycles contain the greatest proportion of REM sleep. In athletes who do not get sufficient hours of sleep, REM sleep can be compromised, reducing neural and psychological performance.

- Identify your sleep requirements and try to get this amount daily.
- Develop a pattern of sleeping and waking times.
- Practice relaxation techniques prior to retiring.
- Try to turn off any worries prior to retiring.
- Make the bedroom as dark as possible, using a mask if necessary.
- Try to maintain a quiet environment, using ear plugs if necessary.
- Use as big a bed as possible (six inches longer than the body is ideal).
- Maintain a cool environment within the bedroom [65° F (18° C) is optimal].
- Keep the head cooler than the body.
- If you don't fall asleep within 30 minutes, get up and do some relaxation work.
- Avoid ingesting caffeine or alcohol in the few hours prior to retiring.

Figure 13-4. Guidelines for sleep enhancement

14

Putting the Program Together

Chapter 5 through 11 of this book outlined how to develop the key fitness attributes required for high-level soccer performance. Knowledge of various training methods is fundamental to setting up effective workout sessions. However, with the wide range of fitness parameters requiring attention, effective planning of the training program is vital if the athlete is to achieve optimal returns.

The fitness-fatigue theory covered in Chapter 2 states that following a training session a rise in fitness level takes place, but accompanied by a rise in fatigue. If the athlete tries to maximally develop all of the fitness parameters at the same time, then the high level of fatigue will result in suboptimal progress, and if continued over time will likely result in a risk of underrecovery and suboptimal performance gains. Therefore, it is important to target specific aspects of fitness at various times throughout the training year. Periodization is a system by which the training year (i.e., the macrocycle) is divided into a number of training periods (i.e. the mesocycles), each with a specific training aim. The training type, volume, and intensity are manipulated throughout the mesocycles to allow for the optimal sequencing of training. The manipulation of training loads to optimize performance can be planned on a number of levels, all of which contribute to the process of periodization.

Levels of Planning

- At the simplest level is the individual training session or bout. This session may be devoted to a single fitness parameter or to a range of parameters. It may take the form of a specific conditioning session or be a part of a larger session (e.g., a speed-based session prior to the commencement of the soccer session).

- At the next level is the training day. In some instances, the athlete may perform a number of sessions during a training day. These sessions need to be planned to effectively sequence the training goals and to optimize recovery between the sessions.

- At the third level is the microcycle, which consists of a collection of several training days, which are often planned on a weekly basis.

- At the fourth level is the mesocycle, which is a period of training, ranging from three to six weeks in length, with a number of key aims. A mesocycle is the collection of a number of microcycles, representing an accumulated period of training.

- At the final level is the macrocycle, normally defined as an entire competition season, normally a single year. For some sports (e.g., Olympic sports), the macrocycle may be four years in duration.

Mesocycle Distribution

Three types of mesocycles can be identified, and the aims of each vary considerably. As a result, the distribution and methods of training also vary.

- Accumulative: The goal is to undertake a period of training aimed at developing one or more fitness parameters. The goal is not peak performance, but simply to undertake the training, upon which future performance will be based.

- Transmutational: The goal is to transfer general fitness into specific game preparedness.

- Realizational: Peaking cycles during which the aim is to achieve peak performance at a given date.

The relative distribution of each of the three types of mesocycle will depend upon both the athlete's developmental stage and the stage of the macrocycle. Athletes in the base stages should focus on developing their fitness within a long-term development model. Therefore, they should predominantly use accumulative mesocycles, as the aim at this stage is to develop a high level of fitness, not necessarily to peak for game performance.

As the athlete moves through the development stage and into the peak stage, the number of transmutative and realizational mesocycles used within a training year will generally increase with each subsequent macrocycle. This shift reflects the move from a focus on base of fitness to training for peak performance. Two key factors must be addressed when developing programs for more advanced athletes:

- The more advanced an athlete, the greater the training impulse required to elicit higher levels of performance
- The more advanced an athlete, the greater the need for variety within the training program

Therefore, more sophisticated periodization systems need to be designed as an athlete becomes more advanced. In addition, the distribution of each type of mesocycle will vary within the macrocycle. In the early phases of the training year, training needs to develop overall fitness and accumulative mesocycles must predominate. As competition approaches, the athlete needs to be able to transmute (i.e., change) this increased fitness into improved on-field performance, and transmutative mesocycles will increase during the precompetition and competition phases. Realizational mesocycles are the least common, and only occur close to major competitions, when peak performance is required. In soccer, realizational mesocycles may coincide with cup finals, playoffs, or major tournaments.

Types of Loads

Understanding different types of loads is key when planning the training year. Three types of loads are utilized in developing periodized training schedules. These loads are based upon a neutral zone load, which is the load required to simply maintain a given state of fitness. With a neutral zone load, levels of fitness will neither improve nor decline.

Stimulating loads—These loads are aimed at enhancing a specific fitness variable. They tend to be above the neutral zone, thus providing overload and forcing the body to adapt. Stimulating loads are normally significantly greater than retaining loads, and so cannot be used on all fitness variables at the same time.

Retaining loads—These loads aim to maintain the level of a fitness variable, rather than develop it. They are well below stimulating loads, and fall in the neutral zone. Retaining loads allow for the maintenance of certain fitness variables within a mesocycle, while stimulating loads are developing others.

Detraining loads—These loads are below the neutral zone and result in a reduction in performance capabilities. Ideally, athletes should avoid these loads whenever possible.

Prioritizing Training Aims

Despite the fact that soccer requires the development of a large range of fitness variables, training is most effective when the number of variables targeted within a micro- and mesocycle is limited to two or three. It is important, therefore, that each micro- and mesocycle has a specific aim in terms of which variables are to be developed. The periodized programs outlined in this chapter take this concept into account, and the allocations of stimulating and retaining loads within each cycle dictate the relative aim of each cycle.

Microcycle Planning

Planning the microcycle revolves around maximizing the return on training while minimizing the effects of fatigue. The aim is to get as much quality training performed in a nonfatigued state as possible. A key element is that fatigue is specific to the type of training undertaken. Therefore, if an athlete performs a heavy strength session for the lower body on Monday, he would still be able to complete a heavy upper-body session on Tuesday.

Another key factor in planning the microcycle is that certain fitness variables are best performed in a nonfatigued state. These variables, which include speed, agility, and explosive power, must be scheduled early in a workout. Similarly, if a number of variables are to be developed in a day, it is best to split them into two shorter sessions, rather than address them in one long session. This format facilitates enhanced hormonal adaptation as well as reduced fatigue within each session, thereby enhancing performance.

Mesocycle Planning

According to renowned sport scientist Vladimir Zatsiorsky, effective planning of training on a medium-term (mesocycle) and long-term (macrocycle) basis depends upon the following four key principles.

Delayed transformation—This principle entails the transformation of the training load into improved performance. Peak performance will not normally occur during periods of heavy training due to the accumulation of training fatigue and the time that adaptation to a training load requires. Thus, a period of easier exercise is needed to demonstrate the results of previous training. A realization mesocycle is needed prior to the main competition to optimize the transfer of the previous training into performance. While this planning is easy in individual sports such as track and field, it is far more difficult in team sports such as soccer in which peak performance needs to be elicited on numerous occasions within a season. The programs outlined in this chapter utilize transition and realization cycles to capitalize on this phenomenon.

Delayed transmutation—Training routines need to be adapted, both in terms of loads and exercises, to transmute the fitness acquired via accumulative mesocycles into enhanced athletic performance. During these periods, exercises are selected that maximize the effects of previous training. A good example is the use of the Olympic lifts after a base of strength has been developed. The effects of the squats and dead lifts performed previously are transmutated into effective Olympic lifting and its associated power development. Performance using this technique is greater than if the Olympic lifts are performed in isolation throughout the training period. Such training tends to be very specific and occurs in the transmutational and realizational mesocycles.

Training residuals—While the "use it or lose it" maxim or reversibility is true, the rate of loss is dependent upon the type of fitness variable (e.g., maximal strength is maintained more effectively than anaerobic endurance) and the length of time taken to develop that parameter. Experienced athletes who have a long history of training take longer to lose fitness than athletes without a long training history. This fact again stresses the need for athletes in the base and development phases to accumulate a large training base, as well as the need for accumulative mesocycles to predominate. Training residuals also allow for retaining loads to be utilized to maintain specific fitness parameters at certain times of the year.

Superposition of training effects—Developing one fitness parameter can have a positive or negative effect on other fitness variables. Training needs to be sequenced to ensure that work in subsequent mesocycles enhances the work carried out in previous mesocycles. For example, strength-training cycles need to precede endurance-training cycles for optimal results.

Types of Periodization

While a huge number of periodization systems are available, they generally can be classified into two types: linear and nonlinear.

Linear periodization—This type of periodization is often called classical periodization. It is the system of dividing the year into a series of blocks normally called general preparatory, specific preparatory, competition, and transition. As the athlete moves through each block, the training becomes more specific, the volume of training tends to decrease, and the intensity increases until the competition taper occurs. This system is most appropriate with sports that involve a clearly identifiable peak and a relatively long off-season, such as track and field.

Nonlinear periodization—Team sports, including soccer, do not effectively fit into the linear periodization model, and so nonlinear periodization is more suitable to developing soccer performance. This type of periodization involves a greater degree of fluctuation within the training year, and within all levels of training cycles. Rather than have a general build-up throughout the year, training fluctuates, aiming to provide for more consistent performance over a longer period of time, as is required during a soccer season. The majority of fitness variables are addressed within all mesocycles, but the emphasis changes on a regular basis and often the use of stimulating and retaining loads varies between cycles. In this way, all of the major fitness requirements of soccer can be addressed, while the fatigue associated with developing or maintaining all of these requirements is controlled.

Dividing the Training Year

A number of methods can be used to divide the training year. The chosen method will largely be dictated by the length of the competition period and the time available for preparation. In general, the following training phases are identifiable within periodized programs.

The aim of each training phase will depend upon the training status of the athlete. As has been stressed throughout this book, athletes in the base phase need to focus on developing a solid foundation of technique and fitness, and therefore will use predominantly accumulative mesocycles. Athletes in the peak phase, on the other hand, will be focusing on maximal performance and will utilize transmutational and realization mesocycles as appropriate.

The Transition Phase

This phase occurs immediately after the season and can be summarized by the term "active recovery." As this phrase suggests, the aim is to enable the athlete to recover from the previous season, physiologically, psychologically and emotionally. It is important that the athlete maintains a degree of physical fitness to prepare him for the off-season preparation cycles. Cross-training workouts and activities away from soccer are ideal at this time. The duration of this period varies from two to four weeks, and is dependent upon the length of the season, the degree of fatigue of the player, and the duration of the entire off-season. As playing seasons have gotten longer, especially in Europe, and the off-seasons progressively shorter, the temptation is to omit this phase completely. This temptation should be resisted, as the transition phase is vital in the athlete's overall program, and is essential for long-term health and performance.

The Off-Season Phase

The off-season phase is the key phase for conditioning. No match commitments exist, so it is easier to achieve the volumes and intensities of training to achieve increases in fitness. Off-season cycles are best divided into four-week blocks. The earlier blocks need to emphasize the individual athlete's weaknesses, working with stimulating loads on no more that two or three fitness variables. These cycles normally represent the highest volume of training and are therefore ideal times to develop weaknesses. At all times, other fitness variables should be maintained via maintenance loads.

In general, with each successive four-week cycle, a general increase in training intensity occurs, as well as a reduction in overall training volume. Skill-training volume, on the other hand, will increase through these cycles as the season approaches.

The Preseason Phase

The preseason phase is essentially the final off-season cycle. It can be a separate cycle or be added to an off-season cycle. The preseason phase is a time when the athlete is being prepared for competition. Training will be of higher intensity and more soccer-specific. Skill training will be at its peak and conditioning training will emphasize the factors that will bring the greatest performance benefits for the player and the team.

The In Season/Competition Phase

The length of the season and the number of games per week will largely dictate the training performed at this stage. The key during a season is to provide training volumes and intensities that maintain the key fitness parameters developed during the off-season, while also minimizing fatigue to allow for high-quality game performance.

A key element of this phase is the use of the summative microcycle system, which allows for a limited number of target parameters per week. It is impossible to address all of the key fitness variables and provide sufficient stimulus to develop them appropriately within one week of training. Limiting the number of parameters allows each one to be given a stimulating load once every four weeks, followed by maintenance loads. This design also minimizes fatigue.

The Training Programs

The programs outlined in this chapter predominantly apply to athletes at the development and peak stages. Modifications are outlined for athletes at the base stage, who are following long-term development programs and utilizing predominantly accumulative cycles. It is important that the athlete has mastered any base-level requirements prior to undertaking these workouts. If mastery has not been achieved, the programs should be adapted to reflect the athlete's needs at this stage.

Dates are not provided, as soccer seasons vary between countries, within countries, and between levels of performance. Therefore, a coach will need to begin at the start of the season and count back in four-week cycles.

In-season mesocycles (competition) are four weeks long and should be repeated through the season, ideally with a higher intensity of training allocated to the workouts with each successive cycle. A week-long transition cycle is recommended to facilitate regeneration after two in-season cycles have been completed.

The realization cycle is a two-week taper cycle and should only be implemented when preparing for the peak of the season. It is best implemented after week 3 of the in-season cycle.

Supplementary Training

Medicine ball work, core strength training, and plyometric training are important parts of the conditioning process. While each may warrant a separate session, within this program they are incorporated into the resistance-training sessions.

Medicine ball throws can either be supersetted with upper-body exercises to provide a contrast, or be used as very dynamic warm-up movements prior to the resistance-training workouts. Similarly, plyometric work can be supersetted with lower-body resistance exercise to facilitate the potentiation effects of resistance exercises, or it can be used as a dynamic warm-up. A suitable way to incorporate the plyometric work would be to perform the short-response drills as a warm-up and have the long-response drills supersetted with the lower-body resistance exercises. Core exercises are listed within the resistance-training program and will normally incorporate exercises that address static holds, movements, and rotation patterns.

Transition Cycle 1

(Figure 14-1)

Objective

The major aim of this cycle is to provide active recovery from the previous season. This recovery takes the form of regeneration on a physiological and psychological basis. All athletes, whatever their stage of development, should be advised to maintain a certain level of activity. Ideally, this activity would involve activities away from their sport and their normal training environment. This change provides psychological recovery from structured workouts in the same environment.

TRAINING PHASE: TRANSITION CYCLE 1

		WEEKS	1 to 3	EMPHASIS	Active recovery

MONDAY	TUESDAY	WEDNESDAY	THURSDAY	FRIDAY	SATURDAY	SUNDAY
Strength 1	Running 1	Regeneration 1	Strength 2	Running 2	Regeneration 2	Off

STRENGTH SESSION 1

Exercise	Week 1	Week 2	Week 3	Week 4
Single-leg squat	3 x 8-10	3 x 8-10	3 x 8-10	
Hamstring lowers	3 x 8-10	3 x 8-10	3 x 8-10	
Push-ups	3 x 8-10	3 x 8-10	3 x 8-10	
Chin-ups	3 x 8-10	3 x 8-10	3 x 8-10	
Plank	2 x 20 sec	2 x 20 sec	2 x 25 sec	
Side bridge	2 x 25 sec	2 x 25 sec	2 x 25 sec	

STRENGTH SESSION 2

Exercise	Week 1	Week 2	Week 3	Week 4
Single-leg squat	3 x 8-10	3 x 8-10	3 x 8-10	
Hamstring lowers	3 x 8-10	3 x 8-10	3 x 8-10	
Push-ups	3 x 8-10	3 x 8-10	3 x 8-10	
Contralateral pull	3 x 8-10	3 x 8-10	3 x 8-10	
Cable chop	2 x 10	2 x 10	2 x 10	

RUNNING SESSION 1
40 minutes general conditioning
Participate in another sport

RUNNING SESSION 2
40 minutes general conditioning
Participate in another sport

STRENGTH SESSION 3

Exercise	Week 1	Week 2	Week 3	Week 4

STRENGTH SESSION 4

Exercise	Week 1	Week 2	Week 3	Week 4

REGENERATION 1
Pool session

REGENERATION 2
Stretching session

Figure 14-1

Resistance-Training Workouts

Resistance-training workouts predominantly employ body weight- or band-based exercises, which can be carried out away from the gym. These exercises will help maintain a certain degree of strength, but negate the need to visit the gym at this time. Exercise will be performed in a controlled manner, accentuating the eccentric portion of the exercise.

Running Workouts

No specific running workouts are recommended at this time. Instead, the athlete is encouraged to take part in other activities that will help maintain running endurance, speed, and agility, but will provide for a more stimulating environment to facilitate regeneration. Tennis and basketball provide examples of suitable activities for this phase.

Regeneration

The stretching workouts have an important role in both facilitating regeneration and maintaining and developing range of motion in key joints and muscle actions. Any key range-of-motion limitations can be addressed at this time.

Off-Season—Phase 1
(Figure 14-2)

Objective

This period is the best time for athletes to work on their weaknesses. It is normally preceded by a fitness-testing program in which any key weaknesses will be highlighted. These weaknesses will then be given stimulating loads, while other fitness variable will be allocated maintenance loads. Given a well-balanced athlete, this phase is normally a hypertrophy phase, and workouts are scheduled and planned to maximize hypertrophy while allowing for the maintenance of other fitness variables.

Resistance-Training Workouts

Exercises—Exercises that stress the greatest amount of muscle mass predominate. Therefore, multijoint exercises that stress the key mobilizing movements of soccer are performed. Exercises are predominantly bilateral, but this phase also includes a small number of unilateral exercises, as many soccer actions are initiated off one foot.

Workout schedules—Three whole-body workouts are scheduled at this time because this program is optimal for developing muscle mass. Session 1 is the heavy day that stresses basic exercises such as the squat, dead lift, bench press, and bent row. Session 2 is the

TRAINING PHASE: OFF-SEASON PHASE 1

MONDAY	TUESDAY	WEDNESDAY	THURSDAY	WEEKS	FRIDAY	EMPHASIS	SATURDAY	SUNDAY
Strength 1 (heavy)	Running 1	Strength 2 (light) (am) Regeneration 1 (pm)	Running 2	4 to 7	Strength 3 (moderate)	Hypertrophy/aerobic endurance	Running 3 (weeks 6 & 7 only)	Regeneration 2

STRENGTH SESSION 1

Exercise	Week 1	Week 2	Week 3	Week 4
Squat	3 x 8-10	3 x 8-10	3 x 8-10	3x 8-10
Dead lift	3 x 6	3 x 6	3 x 6	3 x 6
RDL	3 x 8-10	3 x 8-10	3 x 8-10	3x 8-10
Calf raise	3 x 8-10	3 x 8-10	3 x 8-10	3x 8-10
Bench press	3 x 8-10	3 x 8-10	3 x 8-10	3x 8-10
Bent row	3 x 8-10	3 x 8-10	3 x 8-10	3x 8-10
Plank*	2 x 25 sec	2 x 25 sec	2 x 30 sec	2 x 30 sec
Side bridge*	2 x 25 sec	2 x 25 sec	2 x 30 sec	2 x 30 sec
Cable lift	2 x 10	2 x 10	2 x 10	2 x 10

*Performed on the floor

STRENGTH SESSION 2

Exercise	Week 1	Week 2	Week 3	Week 4
Lunge	3 x 8-10	3 x 8-10	3 x 8-10	3 x 8-10
Single-leg RDL	3 x 8-10	3 x 8-10	3 x 8-10	3 x 8-10
Incline dumbell press	3 x 8-10	3 x 8-10	3 x 8-10	3 x 8-10
Contralateral pull	3 x 8-10	3 x 8-10	3 x 8-10	3 x 8-10
Upright row	3 x 8-10	3 x 8-10	3 x 8-10	3 x 8-10
Cable chop	2 x 10	2 x 10	2 x 10	2 x 10
Bridge	2 x 20 sec	2 x 20 sec	2 x 25 sec	2 x 25 sec
Reverse bridge	2 x 20 sec	2 x 20 sec	2 x 25 sec	2 x 25 sec
Side bridge*	2 x 25 sec	2 x 25 sec	2 x 30 sec	2 x 30 sec

*Performed on the floor

STRENGTH SESSION 3

Exercise	Week 1	Week 2	Week 3	Week 4
Leg press	3 x 8-10	3 x 8-10	3 x 8-10	3 x 8-10
Glute ham	3 x 8-10	3 x 8-10	3 x 8-10	3 x 8-10
Incline dumbbell press	3 x 8-10	3 x 8-10	3 x 8-10	3 x 8-10
Pulley row	3 x 8-10	3 x 8-10	3 x 8-10	3 x 8-10
Shoulder press	3 x 8-10	3 x 8-10	3 x 8-10	3 x 8-10

STRENGTH SESSION 4

Exercise	Week 1	Week 2	Week 3	Week 4

RUNNING SESSION 1

Linear speed & aerobic endurance
- Dynamic warm-up
- Sprint drills (10 minutes)
- Acceleration runs (5 x 60 meters)
- 8 x 2 minutes - level 3/4 endurance game 1:1 work/rest

RUNNING SESSION 2

Agility
- Dynamic warm-up
- Agility technical drills (15 minutes)
- Closed agility drills (20 minutes)

RUNNING SESSION 3

Endurance
- Dynamic warm-up
- 10 x 2 minutes - level 3/4 endurance game

REGENERATION 1

Stretching session

REGENERATION 2

Pool session

RDL= Romanian dead lift

Figure 14-2

light session in which variety is provided via the use of unilateral exercises, which provide for more functional strength development. Session 3 is a moderate session with a similar exercise emphasis as Session 1.

Loads—Loads are selected that will allow for the completion of the established repetition ranges. Momentary muscular failure should occur within these repetition ranges.

Sets/reps—A moderate number of sets (three or four) is performed, utilizing moderate numbers of repetitions (eight to 10). These combinations are optimal for muscle hypertrophy.

Exercise protocols and repetition cadence—Exercises are performed in a slow and controlled manner to keep the tension on the working muscles.

Rest between sets—Rest between sets is short (60 seconds) to stimulate the hormonal adaptations associated with muscle hypertrophy.

Running Workouts

Speed and agility—Technique is the major aim of the speed and agility sessions at this stage. Some high-speed work is carried out, but merely for the maintenance of those aspects of the neuromuscular system associated with speed and agility.

Endurance—One session per week of endurance training is carried out for the first two weeks, focusing on Level 3 /4 work (refer to Chapter 10 for an explanation of work levels). This work is achieved via the use of appropriate small-sided games to better simulate the requirements of soccer. In weeks 6 and 7, an additional endurance session is introduced. Care must be taken at this time not to overload the athlete with endurance stimuli, which can be counterproductive to the development of muscular hypertrophy. For this reason, endurance work is limited to one session per week for the first two weeks.

Supplementary Work

Core-strength work is added to the resistance-training sessions. The exercises selected are aimed at developing the ability to hold positions in both stable and unstable environments.

Modifications for base-level athletes—Technique must dominate this stage for all types of exercise. Therefore, loads will be lower to allow for mastery of technique. Body-weight exercises may still dominate the strength sessions, noncompetitive speed and agility drills will dominate the running sessions, and the core sessions will involve the mastery of the neutral spine and the its development in a stable environment.

Off-Season—Phase 2

(Figure 14-3)

Objective

This period is another key time for athletes to work on their weaknesses, but with other fitness variables given a higher priority depending upon the individuals' scores. Given a well-balanced athlete, this phase is normally allocated as the strength phase, and workouts are scheduled and planned to maximize strength while allowing for the maintenance of other fitness variables. A secondary focus is given to endurance, with an emphasis on high-level aerobic and anaerobic endurance.

Resistance-Training Workouts

Exercises—Exercises that stress the greatest amount of muscle mass and allow for the generation of the greatest force output predominate. Therefore, multijoint exercises that stress the key mobilizing movements for soccer are essential. Unilateral exercises are included to develop force-producing capabilities off one foot. Explosive exercises are included at this time to hone the technique required, before they predominate in off-season phase 4.

Workout schedules—Due to the increased lifting volume, at this point the schedules include four lifting days, with an upper- and lower-body split. Session 1 is the heavy day for lower body and stresses basic exercises such as the squat and deadlift. Session 3 is the light session for the lower body and variety is provided via the use of unilateral exercises, which provide for more functional strength development. Session 2 is the light session for the upper body, while session 4 is the heavy session for the upper body.

Loads—Loads are selected that require the use of a high percentage of one-repetition maximum (1 RM), which is more conducive to strength development.

Sets/reps—A moderate number of sets (three or four) are performed utilizing a low to moderate number of repetitions (six to eight). These combinations reflect the move form a hypertrophy emphasis to a strength emphasis.

Exercise protocols and repetition cadence—Exercises are performed so that the eccentric phase is done in a slow and controlled manner, while the athlete tries to move explosively through the concentric phase. Despite this aim to move explosively, the high resistance will result in a relatively slow movement speed. Nevertheless, the intention should be to move explosively.

Rest between sets—Rest between sets is long (three minutes or more) to allow for maximal forces on subsequent sets.

TRAINING PHASE: OFF-SEASON PHASE 2 | WEEKS 8 to 11 | EMPHASIS — Strength and aerobic/anaerobic endurance

MONDAY	TUESDAY	WEDNESDAY	THURSDAY	FRIDAY	SATURDAY	SUNDAY
Strength 1 (heavy lower body)	Strength 2 (light upper body) Running 1 (pm)	Running 2 am Regeneration 1 (pm)	Strength 3 (light lower body)	Strength 4 (heavy upper body)	Running 3 (weeks 8 & 9 only)	Regeneration 2

STRENGTH SESSION 1

Exercise	Week 1	Week 2	Week 3	Week 4
Hang clean			3 x 4	3 x 4
Squat	4 x 6	4 x 6	4 x 6	4 x 6
Dead lift	3 x 4	3 x 4	3 x 4	3 x 4
RDL	3 x 6	3 x 6	3 x 6	3 x 6
Calf raise	3 x 8	3 x 8	3 x 8	3 x 8

STRENGTH SESSION 2

Exercise	Week 1	Week 2	Week 3	Week 4
Bench press	3 x 6	3 x 6	3 x 6	3 x 6
Bent row	3 x 6	3 x 6	3 x 6	3 x 6
Upright row	3 x 6	3 x 6	3 x 6	3 x 6
Ball ramp	2 x 25 sec	2 x 25 sec	2 x 30 sec	2 x 30 sec
Log roll	2 x 10	2 x 10	2 x 10	2 x 10
Cable lift	2 x 8	2 x 8	2 x 8	2 x 8
Reverse bridge	2 x 25 sec	2 x 25 sec	2 x 30 sec	2 x 30 sec

STRENGTH SESSION 3

Exercise	Week 1	Week 2	Week 3	Week 4
Hang snatch				
Squat	3 x 6	3 x 6	2 x 8	2 x 8
Single-leg squat	2 x 8	2 x 8	2 x 8	2 x 8
Glute hams	3 x 6	3 x 6	3 x 6	3 x 6
Lateral lunges	1 x 10	1 x 10	2 x 10	2 x 10

STRENGTH SESSION 4

Exercise	Week 1	Week 2	Week 3	Week 4
Incline dumbbell press	3 x 6	3 x 6	3 x 6	3 x 6
Pulley row	3 x 8-10	3 x 8-10	3 x 8-10	3 x 8-10
Shoulder press	3 x 8-10	3 x 8-10	3 x 8-10	3 x 8-10
Pull-ins	2 x 10	2 x 10	2 x 10	2 x 10
NSEW	2 x 10	2 x 10	2 x 10	2 x 10
Torso twists	2 x 10	2 x 10	2 x 10	2 x 10
Cable chop	2 x 8	2 x 8	2 x 8	2 x 8

RUNNING SESSION 1

Linear speed & aerobic endurance
- Dynamic warm-up
- Sprint drills (10 minutes)
- Acceleration runs (4 x 60 metes)
- 4 x 40 yards (varied starts)
- 8 x 1.5 minutes - level 4/5 endurance game 1:2 work rest

RUNNING SESSION 2

Agility
- Dynamic warm-up
- Agility technical drills (15 minutes)
- Closed agility drills (20 minutes)

RUNNING SESSION 3

Endurance
- Dynamic warm-up
- 6 x 200-yard runs

Notes:
- 2.5 minutes recovery between reps

REGENERATION 1

Stretching session

REGENERATION 2

Pool session

RDL= Romanian dead lift

NSEW= North, south, east, west

Figure 14-3

Running Workout

Speed and agility—While technique is still the major aim of both the speed and agility sessions at this stage, a greater amount of high-speed running is performed. Where sprints are programmed, they should incorporate running curved patterns as well as straight patterns. Agility sessions involve the transfer of sound technique to closed agility drills, with the emphasis on the transfer of technique to increasingly complex and competitive movements.

Endurance—Two sessions per week of endurance are carried out for the first two weeks of this phase. Session 1 focuses on Level 4/5 work and is achieved via the use of appropriate small-sided games to better simulate the requirements of soccer. Session 2 focuses on the anaerobic glycolytic (lactic) energy system to develop the ability to tolerate and clear lactic acid buildup.

Supplementary Work

Core-strength work is added to the resistance-training sessions. The exercises selected are aimed at developing the ability to both hold positions and produce movement in an unstable environment.

Modifications for Base-Level Athletes

Technique must again dominate this stage for all types of exercise. Loads must be lower to allow for mastery of technique and will follow the hypertrophy repetition range. Body-weight exercises may still dominate the strength sessions, but with basic exercises added. Noncompetitive speed and agility drills will again dominate the running sessions, while the core sessions will involve the mastery of the neutral spine and its development in a stable environment.

Transition Cycle 2

(Figure 14-4)

Objective

Following two training cycles, a degree of fatigue will be present. The major aim in this phase is to provide active recovery from the previous two cycles. This recovery takes the form of regeneration on a physiological and psychological basis.

Resistance-Training Workouts

These workouts will be of a reduced volume (two per week). Session 1 will have a strength emphasis, but with a far lower volume than in the previous mesocycles,

TRAINING PHASE: TRANSITION CYCLE 2 — WEEK 12 — EMPHASIS

MONDAY	TUESDAY	WEDNESDAY	THURSDAY	FRIDAY	SATURDAY	SUNDAY
Strength 1	Running 1	Regeneration 1	Strength 2	Off	Regeneration 2	Off
						Active recovery

STRENGTH SESSION 1

Exercise	Week 1	Week 2	Week 3	Week 4
Squat	2 x 6			
RDL	2 x 6			
Bench Press	2 x 6			
Bent row	2 x 6			
Brdge	1 x 30 sec			
Side bridge	1 x 30 sec			
Cable lift	2 x 10			

STRENGTH SESSION 2

Exercise	Week 1	Week 2	Week 3	Week 4
Single-leg squat	2 x 8-10			
Single-leg RDL	2 x 8-10			
Incline dumbbell press	2 x 8-10			
Contralateral pull	2 x 8-10			
Cable chop	1 x 10			
Bridge	1 x 30 sec			
Reverse bridge	1 x 30 sec			

STRENGTH SESSION 3

Exercise	Week 1	Week 2	Week 3	Week 4

STRENGTH SESSION 4

Exercise	Week 1	Week 2	Week 3	Week 4

RUNNING SESSION 1

RUNNING SESSION 2

REGENERATION 1

Pool workout

REGENERATION 2

Stretching workout

RDL= Romanian dead lift

Figure 14-4

reflecting the recovery aim of the cycle. Session 2 will emphasize hypertrophy and functional strength and will be the lighter session of the two.

Running Workouts

No specific running workouts are programmed at this time. Instead, the athlete will be taking part in team practices, which will maintain the key fitness variables.

Regeneration

The stretching workouts have an important role in both facilitating regeneration and maintaining and developing range of motion in key joints and muscle actions.

Off-Season—Phase 3
(Figure 14-5)

Objective

In this phase, the emphasis moves from general preparation to more specific preparation, and key game elements such as peak strength, power, speed, and agility play a more prominent role in the conditioning process. This phase is normally allocated as the peak strength phase, and workouts are scheduled and planned to maximize this variable while allowing for the maintenance of other fitness variables. A secondary focus is given to anaerobic endurance.

Resistance-Training Workouts

Exercises—Exercises that stress the greatest amount of muscle mass and allow for the generation of the greatest force output predominate. Therefore, multijoint exercises that stress the key mobilizing movements for soccer must be performed. Unilateral exercises are included to develop force-producing capabilities off one foot. Explosive exercises are included at this time to start the process of developing rapid rates of force development.

Workout schedules—Routines continue with an upper- and lower-body split. Session 1 is the heavy day for the lower body and stresses basic exercises. Session 3 is the light session for the lower body and variety is provided via the use of unilateral exercises, which provide for more functional strength development. Session 2 is the light session for the upper body, while session 4 is the heavy session for the upper body.

Loads—Loads are selected that require the use of a high percentage of 1 RM, which is more conducive to strength development.

TRAINING PHASE: OFF-SEASON PHASE 3				WEEKS 13 to 16	EMPHASIS	Strength and anaerobic endurance
MONDAY	TUESDAY	WEDNESDAY	THURSDAY	FRIDAY	SATURDAY	SUNDAY
Strength 1 (heavy lower body)	Strength 2 (light upper body); Running 1 pm	Running 2 (am); Regeneration 1 (pm)	Strength 3 (light lower body)	Strength 4 (heavy upper body)	Running 3 (weeks 15 & 16 only)	Regeneration 2

STRENGTH SESSION 1

Exercise	Week 1	Week 2	Week 3	Week 4
Hang clean	3 x 4	3 x 4	4 x 3	4 x 3
Squat	4 x 4	4 x 4	4 x 4	4 x 4
Dead lift	3 x 3	3 x 3	3 x 2	3 x 2
RDL	3 x 4	3 x 4	3 x 4	3 x 4
Calf raise	3 x 8	3 x 8	3 x 8	3 x 8

Squats supersetted with plyometrics in weeks 15 & 16

STRENGTH SESSION 2

Exercise	Week 1	Week 2	Week 3	Week 4
Bench press	3 x 4	3 x 4	3 x 4	3 x 4
Bent row	3 x 4	3 x 4	3 x 4	3 x 4
Upright row	3 x 4	3 x 4	3 x 4	3 x 4
Reverse ramp	2 x 30 sec	2 x 30 sec	2 x 30 sec	2 x 30 sec
Log roll	2 x 10	2 x 10	2 x 10	2 x 10
Cable lift	2 x 8	2 x 8	2 x 8	2 x 8
Reverse bridge	2 x 30 sec	2 x 30 sec	2 x 30 sec	2 x 30 sec

Upper-body exercises supersetted with medicine ball throws in weeks 15 & 16

STRENGTH SESSION 3

Exercise	Week 1	Week 2	Week 3	Week 4
Hang snatch	3 x 4	3 x 4	4 x 3	4 x 3
Squat	3 x 4	3 x 4	3 x 6	3 x 6
Single-leg squat	2 x 5	2 x 5	2 x 5	2 x 5
Glute hams	3 x 6	3 x 6	3 x 6	3 x 6
Lateral lunge	2 x 8	2 x 8	2 x 6	2 x 6

STRENGTH SESSION 4

Exercise	Week 1	Week 2	Week 3	Week 4
Incline dumbbell press	3 x 6	3 x 6	3 x 6	3 x 6
Pulley row	3 x 8-10	3 x 8-10	3 x 8-10	3 x 8-10
Shoulder press	3 x 8-10	3 x 8-10	3 x 8-10	3 x 8-10
Elbow crunches	2 x 10	2 x 10	2 x 10	2 x 10
NSEW	2 x 10	2 x 10	2 x 10	2 x 10
Skiers	2 x 10	2 x 10	2 x 10	2 x 10
Cable chop	2 x 8	2 x 8	2 x 8	2 x 8

RUNNING SESSION 1

Linear speed & aerobic endurance
- Dynamic warm-up
- Sprint drills (10 minutes)
- Acceleration runs (4 x 60 yards)
- 6 x 40 yards (varied starts)
- 8 x 1 minute - level 5 endurance game 1:3 work/rest

RUNNING SESSION 2

Agility
- Dynamic warm-up
- Agility technical drills (15 minutes)
- Closed agility drills (10 minutes)
- Open agility drills (10 minutes)
- Sprint-resisted runs 4 x 20 yards

RUNNING SESSION 3

Endurance
- Dynamic warm-up
- 6 x 60-yard sprints

Notes:
- 30 seconds recovery between reps
- Increase by 2 sprints weekly
- Once at 10 reps, split into 2 sets
- 5 minutes between sets

REGENERATION 1

Stretching session

REGENERATION 2

Pool session

RDL= Romanian dead lift

NSEW= North, south, east, west

Figure 14-5

Sets/reps—A moderate number of sets (three or four) are performed utilizing a low number of repetitions (three to six). These combinations are optimal for developing muscle strength.

Exercise protocols and repetition cadence—Exercises are performed so that the eccentric phase is done in a slow and controlled manner, while the athlete tries to move explosively through the concentric phase. Despite this aim to move explosively, the high resistance will result in a relatively slow movement speed. Nevertheless, the intention should be to move explosively.

Rest between sets—Rest between sets is long (three minutes or more) to allow for maximal forces on subsequent sets.

Running Workouts

Speed and agility—Again, as this phase progresses, a greater amount of high-speed running is carried out. Where sprints are programmed, they should incorporate running curved patterns as well as straight patterns. In addition, sprint-resisted running is introduced. Agility sessions involve the transfer of sound technique to closed agility drills, with the emphasis on the transfer of technique to increasingly complex and competitive movements. Sessions also include open drills at the end.

Endurance—One session per week of endurance is carried out for the first two weeks of this phase. Session 1 focuses on high-intensity Level 5 work, which is again achieved via the use of appropriate small-sided games to better simulate the requirements of soccer. Session 2, which is introduced in the final two weeks, focuses on anaerobic ATP-PCr endurance to develop the ability to repeat high-intensity sprints.

Supplementary Work

Core-strength work is again added to the resistance-training sessions. The exercises selected are aimed at developing the ability to hold positions and increasingly to produce movement in an unstable environment.

Medicine ball work is introduced into the upper-body resistance sessions, and whenever possible, is supersetted with upper-body exercises. Exercises should be selected according to the criteria presented in Chapter 8. Aim for 50 throws by the end of the phase.

Plyometric work is introduced into the resistance-training workouts and is supersetted with lower-body exercises. Selected exercises need to include both short- and long-response exercises, with 40 foot contacts of the former and 40 foot contacts of the latter being achieved by the end of the phase.

Modifications for Base-Level Athletes

Technique must again dominate this stage for all types of exercise. Therefore, loads must be lower to allow for mastery of technique and should follow the hypertrophy repetition range (i.e., eight to 12). Body-weight exercises may still be a part of the strength sessions, but with basic exercises taking a bigger role. Noncompetitive speed and agility drills will again dominate the running sessions, while during the core sessions controlled movements will be developed in a stable environment while maintaining postural integrity. No plyometric work will be performed.

Off-Season—Phase 4

(Figure 14-6)

Objective

The emphasis during this phase becomes even more specific preparation, and key game elements such as power, speed, and agility dominate in the conditioning process. This phase is normally the power phase, and workouts are scheduled and planned to maximize this variable together with speed and agility.

Resistance-Training Workouts

Exercises—Explosive exercises are used to enhance the process of building rapid rates of force development. Strength exercises that stress the greatest amount of muscle mass and allow for the generation of the greatest force output again predominate the strength program. Therefore, multijoint exercises that stress the key mobilizing movements for soccer are performed. Unilateral exercises are included to develop force-producing capabilities off one foot.

Workout schedules—Routines continue with an upper- and lower-body split. Session 1 is the heavy day for the lower body and stresses basic exercises. Session 3 is the light session for the lower body and variety is provided via the use of unilateral exercises, which provide for more functional strength development. Session 2 is the light session for the upper body, while session 4 is the heavy session for the upper body.

Loads—Loads are selected that require the use of a high percentage of 1 RM, which is more conducive to strength development. For explosive exercises, loads are chosen that maximize power output.

Sets/reps—A moderate number of sets (three or four) are performed, utilizing a low number of repetitions (three to six) for strength exercises and a very low number (three) for explosive exercises. These combinations are optimal for the development of muscle strength and power.

Exercise protocols and repetition cadence—Exercises are performed explosively, as the athlete tries to explode through the concentric phase.

Rest between sets—Rest between sets is long (three minutes or more) to allow for the use of maximal force on subsequent sets.

Running Workouts

Speed and agility—As this phase progresses, a greater amount of high-speed running is carried out. Where sprints are programmed, they should incorporate running curved patterns as well as straight patterns. In addition, sprint-resisted running is maintained and sprint-assisted (overspeed) running is introduced to enhance maximal speed. Agility sessions are dominated by high-quality open drills.

Endurance—One session per week of endurance is performed for the first three weeks of this phase. In weeks 17 and 19, ATP-PCr endurance is stressed via repeat sprints. In week 18, the focus is on high-intensity Level 5 work, which is again achieved via the use of appropriate small-sided games to better simulate the requirements of soccer.

Supplementary Work

Core-strength work is again added to the resistance-training sessions. The exercises selected are aimed at developing the ability to hold positions and increasingly to produce movement in an unstable environment. The movements also can become more explosive.

Medicine ball work is included in the upper-body resistance sessions, and, whenever possible, is supersetted with upper-body exercises. Exercises should be selected according to the criteria presented in Chapter 8. Aim for 70 throws by the end of the phase.

Plyometric work is introduced into the resistance-training workouts and is supersetted with lower-body exercises. Selected exercises need to include both short- and long-response exercises, with 60 foot contacts of the former and 60 foot contacts of the latter achieved by the end of the phase. All movements should be of maximum quality.

Modifications for Base-Level Athletes

Technique will again dominate this stage for all types of exercise. Therefore, loads must be lower to allow for mastery of technique and will follow the hypertrophy repetition range. Basic resistance exercises will dominate at this time. Noncompetitive speed and agility drills will again dominate the running sessions, while the core sessions will utilize both a stable and unstable environment for static holds and further develop movement in the stable environment. No plyometric work will be performed.

TRAINING PHASE: OFF-SEASON PHASE 4				WEEKS	17 to 20	EMPHASIS	Power, speed, PCr endurance
MONDAY	TUESDAY	WEDNESDAY	THURSDAY	FRIDAY	SATURDAY		SUNDAY
Strength 1 (explosive & heavy lower body)	Strength 2 (Light upper body) Running 1 (pm)	Running 2 (am) Regeneration 1 (pm)	Strength 3 (explosive & light lower body)	Strength 4 (heavy upper body)	Running 3 (only perform endurance in weeks 17 & 19)		Regeneration 2

STRENGTH SESSION 1

Exercise	Week 1	Week 2	Week 3	Week 4
Hang clean	3 x 3	3 x 4	4 x 3	4 x 3
Snatch	3 x 3	3 x 3	3 x 3	3 x 3
Squat	4 x 4	4 x 4	4 x 4	4 x 4
Dead lift	3 x 3	3 x 3	3 x 3	3 x 3
RDL	3 x 3	3 x 3	3 x 3	3 x 3
Calf raise	3 x 8	3 x 8	3 x 8	3 x 8

Squats supersetted with plyometrics

STRENGTH SESSION 2

Exercise	Week 1	Week 2	Week 3	Week 4
Bench press	3 x 4	3 x 4	3 x 4	3 x 4
Bent row	3 x 4	3 x 4	3 x 4	3 x 4
Upright row	4 x 4	4 x 4	4 x 4	4 x 4
Elbow crunches	2 x 10	2 x 10	2 x 10	2 x 10
Log roll	2 x 10	2 x 10	2 x 10	2 x 10
Cable lift	2 x 8	2 x 8	2 x 8	2 x 8
Reverse bridge	2 x 30 sec	2 x 30 sec	2 x 30 sec	2 x 30 sec
Medicine ball crunch throw	2 x 8	2 x 8	3 x 6	3 x 6

Upper-body exercises supersetted with medicine ball throws

RDL= Romanian dead lift

STRENGTH SESSION 3

Exercise	Week 1	Week 2	Week 3	Week 4
Hang snatch	3 x 4	3 x 4	4 x 3	4 x 3
Power clean	3 x 3	3 x 3	3 x 3	3 x 3
Squat	3 x 4	3 x 4	3 x 6	3 x 6
Single-leg squat	2 x 5	2 x 5	2 x 5	2 x 5
Glute hams	3 x 6	3 x 6	3 x 6	3 x 6

All squats supersetted with pyometrics

STRENGTH SESSION 4

Exercise	Week 1	Week 2	Week 3	Week 4
Incline dumbbell press	3 x 6	3 x 6	3 x 6	3 x 6
Pulley row	3 x 8-10	3 x 8-10	3 x 8-10	3 x 8-10
Shoulder press	3 x 8-10	3 x 8-10	3 x 8-10	3 x 8-10
Ramp	2 x 30 sec	2 x 30 sec	2 x 30 sec	2 x 30 sec
NSEW	2 x 10	2 x 10	2 x 10	2 x 10
Skiers	2 x 10	2 x 10	2 x 10	2 x 10
Cable chop	2 x 8	2 x 8	2 x 8	2 x 8
Medicine ball crunch throw	3 x 6	3 x 6	4 x 6	4 x 6

Upper-body exercises supersetted with medicine ball throws

NSEW= North, south, east, west

RUNNING SESSION 1

Linear speed & aerobic endurance
- Dynamic warm-up
- Sprint drills (10 minutes)
- Assisted runs (5 x 30 yards)
- 6 x 40 yards (varied starts)
- 6 x 1 minute (week 18 only) - level 5 endurance game 1:3 work rest

RUNNING SESSION 2

Agility
- Dynamic warm-up
- Agility technical drills (15 minutes)
- Acceleration runs (6 x 60 yards)
- Closed agility drills (10 minutes)
- Open agility drills (20 minutes)

RUNNING SESSION 3

Speed & endurance
- Dynamic warm-up
- Resisted runs (5 x 30 yards)
- 2 x 6 x 60-yard sprints

Notes:
- 30 seconds recovery between reps
- 10 minutes recovery between sets

REGENERATION 1

Stretching session

REGENERATION 2

Pool session

Figure 14-6

Precompetition

(Figure 14-7)

Objective

This short, two-week realization phase follows immediately after off-season phase four, and is the first transmutational cycle. The goal of this phase is to achieve a high quality of performance during the first game of the season. The emphasis is on an even greater degree of specific preparation, and key game elements such as power, speed, and agility dominate the conditioning process. The volume of work is greatly reduced to allow for regeneration. This phase is normally categorized as the power phase, and workouts are scheduled and planned to maximize this variable together with speed and agility.

Resistance-Training Workouts

Exercises—Explosive exercises dominate at this time to enhance the process of building rapid rates of force development. For strength work, exercises that stress the greatest amount of muscle mass and allow for the generation of the greatest force output again predominate. Therefore, multijoint exercises that stress the key mobilizing movements for soccer are performed. Unilateral exercises are included to develop force-producing capabilities off one foot.

Workout schedules—Routines continue with an upper- and lower-body split. Session 1 is the heavy day for the lower body and stresses basic exercises. Session 3 is the light session for the lower body and variety is provided via the use of unilateral exercises, which provide for more functional strength development. Session 2 is the heavy session for the upper body, while session 4 is the light session for the upper body. Note that the heavy sessions are scheduled for early in the week, facilitating recovery before the weekend games.

Loads—For basic exercises, loads are selected that require the use of a high percentage of 1 RM, which is more conducive to strength development. For explosive exercises, loads are chosen that maximize power output.

Sets/reps—A moderate number of sets (three or four) are performed, utilizing a low number of repetitions (three to six) for strength exercises and a very low number (three) for explosive exercises. These combinations are optimal for the development of muscle strength and power.

Exercise protocols and repetition cadence—Exercises are performed explosively, as the athlete tries to explode through the concentric phase.

Rest between sets—Rest between sets is long (three minutes or more) to allow for the use of maximal force on subsequent sets.

TRAINING PHASE: PRECOMPETITION			WEEKS	21 to 22	EMPHASIS	Peak power & speed
MONDAY	**TUESDAY**	**WEDNESDAY**	**THURSDAY**	**FRIDAY**	**SATURDAY**	**SUNDAY**
Strength 1 (explosive & heavy lower body)	Strength 2 (heavy upper body) Running 1 (pm)	Running 2 (am) Regeneration 1 (pm)	Strength 3 (explosive & light total body)	Regeneration 2	Game	Regeneration 2

STRENGTH SESSION 1

Exercise	*Week 1*	*Week 2*	*Week 3*	*Week 4*
Power clean	3 x 3	3 x 4		
Snatch	3 x 3	3 x 3		
Squat	4 x 4	4 x 4		
RDL	3 x 3	3 x 3		
Calf raise	3 x 8	3 x 8		
Medicine ball crunch throw	4 x 6	4 x 6		
Elbow crunches	2 x 10	2 x 10		
Pikes	2 x 10	2 x 10		
Skiers	2 x 10	2 x 10		
Cable chop	2 x 8	2 x 8		

Squats supersetted with plyometrics

STRENGTH SESSION 2

Exercise	*Week 1*	*Week 2*	*Week 3*	*Week 4*
Bench press	3 x 4	3 x 4		
Bent row	3 x 4	3 x 4		
Shoulder press	3 x 4	3 x 4		
NSEW	2 x 10	2 x 10		
Log roll	2 x 10	2 x 10		
Cable lift	2 x 8	2 x 8		
Reverse bridge	2 x 30 sec	2 x 30 sec		

Upper-body exercises supersetted with medicine ball throws

RDL= Romanian dead lift *NSEW= North, south, east, west*

STRENGTH SESSION 3

Exercise	*Week 1*	*Week 2*	*Week 3*	*Week 4*
Hang clean	3 x 3	3 x 3		
Squat	3 x 4	3 x 4		
Single-leg squat	2 x 5	2 x 5		
Glute hams	3 x 6	3 x 6		
Bench	3 x 4	3 x 3		
Contralateral pulls	3 x 4	3 x 4		

All squats supersetted with plyometrics

All exercises performed explosively

STRENGTH SESSION 4

Exercise	*Week 1*	*Week 2*	*Week 3*	*Week 4*

RUNNING SESSION 1

Linear speed & aerobic endurance
- Dynamic warm-up
- Sprint drills (10 minutes)
- Assisted runs (4 x 30 meters)
- 4 x 40 yards (varied starts)
- 3 x 20 yards sprint resisted runs
- 6 x 1 minute (week 21 only) - level 5 endurance game 1:3 work/rest

RUNNING SESSION 2

Agility
- Dynamic warm-up
- Agility technical drills (15 minutes)
- Asssited runs (5 x 30 meters)
- Closed agility drills (5 minutes)
- Open agility drills (15 minutes)

RUNNING SESSION 3

REGENERATION 1

Stretching session

REGENERATION 2

Pool session

Figure 14-7

Running Workouts

Speed and agility—Quality is paramount at this stage and involves high-speed running whenever sprints are programmed. These sprints should incorporate running curved patterns as well as straight patterns. In addition, sprint-resisted running is maintained and sprint-assisted running continued, with the emphasis falling on the latter. Agility sessions are high-quality and based on open drills.

Endurance—One session per week of endurance training is carried out for the first week only. High-intensity Level 5 work is again utilized via appropriate small-sided games.

Supplementary Work

Core-strength work is again added to the resistance-training sessions. The exercises selected are aimed at developing the ability to hold positions and produce movement—including explosive movement—in an unstable environment.

Medicine ball work is included in the upper-body resistance sessions, and, whenever possible, is supersetted with upper-body exercises. Exercises should be selected according to the criteria presented in Chapter 8.

Plyometric work is included in the resistance-training workouts and is supersetted with lower-body exercises. Selected exercises need to include both short- and long-response exercises, with 40 foot contacts of the former and 40 foot contacts of the latter during this phase. These exercises all should be of maximum quality.

Modifications for Base-Level Athletes

As with all phases of the base program, technique must again dominate this stage for all types of exercise. Therefore, loads must be lower to allow for mastery of technique and will more follow the strength/hypertrophy repetition range. Basic exercises will dominate the sessions. Noncompetitive speed and agility drills will again dominate the running sessions, while the core sessions will utilize both a stable environment and an unstable environment for static holds, together with movement in the stable environment. No plyometric work will be performed.

In-Season Cycles

Objective

The aim of these cycles is to utilize a nonlinear undulating pattern of loading and unloading to ensure that all fitness variables are given both stimulating and maintenance loads within the four-week cycle. At the same time, the sessions must reduce the buildup of accumulated fatigue.

Each week of training has a specific aim, with stimulating loads attached to these aims. Other parameters are then given maintenance loads. Following the four-week cycle, the whole pattern is repeated. The goal is to use a summated microcycle system whereby loads in each subsequent cycle are greater than in the one previous (e.g., if the athlete was lifting 220 pounds in the squat in hypertrophy cycle 1, he may be asked to lift 225 pounds in cycle 2, and so on).

Following two cycles (i.e., eight weeks of training), a transition and regenerating cycle lasting a single week is introduced. The aim of this week is to allow for a more complete recovery from training stresses and for psychological regeneration.

It should be noted that all of the cycles presented are based around a single game per week, played on a Saturday. Programs should be altered appropriately to reflect the competition schedule.

Realization Cycles

At a crucial point of the season, a two-week realization cycle can be introduced. This cycle should be utilized no more than two times per season and needs to coincide with the season's peak (e.g., playoff game). This cycle should be introduced immediately after week 3 of the in-season cycle and not after week 4 (i.e., weeks 1 to 3 of the in-season cycle, followed immediately by the realization cycle).

In-Season Week 1
(Figure 14-8)

Objective

The primary emphasis during this week is muscular hypertrophy.

Resistance-Training Workouts

Exercises—Exercises that stress the greatest amount of muscle mass predominate. Therefore, multijoint exercises that stress the key mobilizing movements for soccer are performed. These exercises are predominantly bilateral but also include unilateral exercises, as many soccer actions are initiated off one foot.

Workout schedules—Four split-body workouts are scheduled at this time. Sessions 1 and 2 are the heavy days and stress basic exercises such as the squat, dead lift, bench press, and bent row. Sessions 3 and 4 are the lighter days, thereby allowing for some recovery before the scheduled game.

Loads—Loads are selected that will allow for the completion of the designated repetition ranges. Momentary muscular failure should occur within these repetition ranges.

TRAINING PHASE: IN-SEASON WEEK 1

MONDAY	TUESDAY	WEDNESDAY	WEEKS THURSDAY	1 FRIDAY	EMPHASIS SATURDAY	SUNDAY
Strength 1 (heavy)	Strength 2 (heavy)	Strength 3 (am)	Strength 4 (light)	Regeneration 1	Game	Regeneration 2
	Running 1	Regeneration 1 (pm)	Running 2 (included in warm-up for technical session)			Hypertrophy

STRENGTH SESSION 1

Exercise	Week 1	Week 2	Week 3	Week 4
Squat	4 x 8-10			
Dead lift	3 x 6			
RDL	3 x 8-10			
Calf raise	3 x 8-10			
Single-leg squat	4 x 8			

STRENGTH SESSION 2

Exercise	Week 1	Week 2	Week 3	Week 4
Bench press	4 x 8			
Bent row	4 x 6			
Upright row	4 x 6			
Pull-ins	2 x 12			
Torso twists	2 x 10			
Cable lift	2 x 8			
Reverse bridge	2 x 25 sec			

STRENGTH SESSION 3

Exercise	Week 1	Week 2	Week 3	Week 4
Hang clean	2 x 3			
Squat	4 x 8			
Glute hams	4 x 8			
Calf raise	4 x 8			

STRENGTH SESSION 4

Exercise	Week 1	Week 2	Week 3	Week 4
Incline dumbbell press	4 x 8			
Pulley row	3 x 8-10			
Shoulder press	3 x 8-10			
Elbow crunches	2 x 10			
NSEW	2 x 10			
Skiers	2 x 10			
Cable chop	2 x 8			

RUNNING SESSION 1

Linear speed & aerobic endurance
- Dynamic warm-up
- Sprint drills (10 minutes)
- Acceleration runs (5 x 60 meters)
- 10 x 2 minutes - level 3/4 endurance game 1:1 work/rest

RUNNING SESSION 2

Agility
- Dynamic warm-up
- Agility technical drills (10 minutes)
- Open agility drills (10 minutes)

RUNNING SESSION 3

REGENERATION 1

Stretching session

REGENERATION 2

Pool session

RDL = Romanian dead lift

NSEW= North, south, east, west

Figure 14-8

Sets/reps—A moderate number of sets (three or four) is performed utilizing a moderate number of repetitions (eight to 10). These combinations are optimal for targeting muscle hypertrophy.

Exercise protocols and repetition cadence—Exercises are performed in a slow and controlled manner to keep the tension on the working muscles.

Rest between sets—Rest between sets is short (about 60 seconds) to stimulate the hormonal adaptations associated with muscle hypertrophy.

Running Workouts

Speed and agility—Speed and agility sessions during this stage are aimed at maintaining a high quality of movement.

Endurance—One session of endurance is carried out, focusing on Level 4 aerobic works.

Supplementary Work

Core-strength work is added to the upper-body resistance-training sessions, with one session working on stabilization and the other on movement in an unstable environment.

Modifications for Base-Level Athletes

Base-level athletes should undertake a block approach similar to the previous off-season phases.

In-Season Week 2
(Figure 14-9)

Objective

The training focus of this week is on maximum strength, with a secondary emphasis on speed and agility.

Resistance-Training Workout

Exercises—As in the off-season strength cycles, exercises that stress the greatest amount of muscle mass and allow for the generation of the greatest force output predominate. Therefore, multijoint exercises that stress the key mobilizing movements for soccer are performed. Unilateral exercises are included to develop force-producing capabilities off one foot. Some explosive exercises are included at this time to maintain the rate of force development.

TRAINING PHASE: IN-SEASON WEEK 2 — **WEEKS 2** — **EMPHASIS Strength**

MONDAY	TUESDAY	WEDNESDAY	THURSDAY	FRIDAY	SATURDAY	SUNDAY
Strength 1 (heavy)	Strength 2 (heavy)	Strength 3 (am) (light)	Strength 4 (light)	Regeneration 1	Game	Regeneration 2
	Running 1	Regeneration 1 (pm)	Running 2			

STRENGTH SESSION 1

Exercise	Week 1	Week 2	Week 3	Week 4
Hang snatch		3 x 3		
Squat		4 x 4-6		
Dead lift		3 x 3		
RDL		4 x 6		
Calf raise		3 x 8		

Plyometrics supersetted into workout

STRENGTH SESSION 2

Exercise	Week 1	Week 2	Week 3	Week 4
Bench press		4 x 4		
Bent row		4 x 4		
Upright row		4 x 4		
Pikes		2 x 10		
Log roll		2 x 10		
Cable lift		2 x 8		
Reverse bridge		2 x 25 sec		

Medicine ball throws supersetted with upper-body exercises

STRENGTH SESSION 3

Exercise	Week 1	Week 2	Week 3	Week 4
Hang clean		2 x 3		
Squat		3 x 8		
Single-leg squat		2 x 8		
Glute hams		4 x 8		
Calf raise		4 x 8		

Plyometrics supersetted into workout

STRENGTH SESSION 4

Exercise	Week 1	Week 2	Week 3	Week 4
Incline dumbbell press		4 x 6		
Pulley row		4 x 6		
Shoulder press		3 x 6		
Elbow crunches		2 x 10		
NSEW		2 x 10		
Skiers		2 x 10		
Cable chop		2 x 8		

Medicine ball throws supersetted with upper-body exercises

NSEW= North, south, east, west

RUNNING SESSION 1

Linear speed & aerobic endurance
· Dynamic warm-up
· Sprint drills (10 minutes)
· Acceleration runs (5 x 60 yards)
· Sprint-resisted runs (5 x 20 yards)
· 2 x 5 x 60 yards (30-second recovery)

RUNNING SESSION 2

Agility
· Dynamic warm-up
· Agility technical drills (10 minutes)
· 4 x 40-yard sprints
· Open agility drills (15 minutes)

RUNNING SESSION 3

REGENERATION 1

Stretching session

REGENERATION 2

Pool session

RDL= Romanian dead lift

Figure 14-9

Workout schedules—Routines continue with an upper- and lower-body split. Session 1 is the heavy day for the lower body and stresses basic exercises. Session 3 is the light session for the lower body and variety is provided via the use of unilateral exercises, which provide for more functional strength development. Session 2 is the heavy session for the upper body, while session 4 is the light session for the upper body.

Loads—Loads are selected that require the use of a high percentage of 1 RM, which is more conducive to strength development.

Sets/reps—A moderate number of sets (three or four) are performed utilizing a low number of repetitions (three to six). These combinations are optimal for the development of muscle strength.

Exercise protocols and repetition cadence—Exercises are performed so that the eccentric phase is done in a slow and controlled manner, while the athlete tries to move explosively through the concentric phase. Despite this aim to move explosively, the high resistance will result in a relatively slow movement speed. Nevertheless, the intention should be to move explosively.

Rest between sets—Rest between sets is long (three minutes or more) to allow for the use of maximal forces on subsequent sets.

Running Workout

Speed and agility—Quality acceleration and maximum-speed work is programmed during this phase. Sprints should incorporate running curved patterns as well as straight patterns. In addition, sprint-resisted running is utilized. Agility sessions involve a mixture of closed and predominantly open agility drills.

Endurance—One session of endurance is carried out early in the week. This session focuses on PCr anaerobic endurance via repeated sprints.

Supplementary Work

Core-strength work is incorporated into the resistance-training sessions. The exercises selected are aimed at developing the ability to hold positions and increasingly to produce movement in an unstable environment.

Medicine ball work is incorporated into the first upper-body resistance sessions, and, whenever possible, is supersetted with upper-body exercises. Exercises should be selected according to the criteria presented in Chapter 8. Fifty throws are programmed in this phase.

Plyometric work is incorporated into the first resistance-training workout and is supersetted with lower-body exercises. Exercises include both short- and long-response exercises, with 40 foot contacts of the former and 40 foot contacts of the latter carried out in these sessions.

In-Season Week 3
(Figure 14-10)

Objective

The development of power, speed, and agility is the main focus for this week.

Resistance-Training Workouts

Exercises—Explosive exercises dominate at this time to enhance the process of building rapid rates of force development.

Workout schedules—Routines revert to a twice-a-week total-body schedule with explosive Olympic lifts predominating.

Loads—Loads are selected that require the use of a high percentage of 1 RM, which is more conducive to strength development. For explosive exercises, loads are chosen that maximize power output.

Sets/reps—A moderate number of sets (three or four) utilizing a low number of repetitions (three) are used for explosive exercises. Other exercises require a low number of sets of few repetitions as maintenance loads.

Exercise protocols and repetition cadence—All exercises are performed explosively.

Rest between sets—Rest between sets is long (three to five minutes or more), to allow for the use of maximal forces on subsequent sets.

Running Workouts

Speed and agility—Speed and agility dominate during this phase, and a moderate volume of high-quality work that focuses on both acceleration and maximum speed is incorporated. Additionally, both assisted and resisted runs are utilized. Agility sessions focus on open drills and high-speed, high-quality movements.

Endurance—No endurance work is performed during this week.

Supplementary Work

Core-strength work is again added to the resistance-training sessions. The exercises

TRAINING PHASE: IN-SEASON WEEK 3

			WEEKS	3	EMPHASIS	Power & speed
MONDAY	**TUESDAY**	**WEDNESDAY**	**THURSDAY**	**FRIDAY**	**SATURDAY**	**SUNDAY**
Strength 1 (heavy)	Running 1	Strength 2 (light) / Regeneration 1 (pm)	Running 2	Regeneration 1	Game	Regeneration 2

STRENGTH SESSION 1

Exercise	Week 1	Week 2	Week 3	Week 4
Clean			4 x 3	
Hang snatch			3 x 3	
Squat			2 x 3	
RDL			2 x 6	
Bench press			2 x 4	
Contralateral rows			2 x 4	
Medicine ball crunch throw			4 x 6	
NSEW			2 x 10	
Skiers			2 x 10	
Cable chop			2 x 8	

Medicine ball throws supersetted with upper-body work

Lower-body work supersetted with plyometrics

STRENGTH SESSION 2

Exercise	Week 1	Week 2	Week 3	Week 4
Snatch			4 x 3	
Hang clean			3 x 3	
Single-leg squats			2 x 5	
Single-leg glute hams			2 x 5	
Incline dumbbell press			2 x 4	
Bent row			2 x 4	
Shoulder press			2 x 4	
Pikes			2 x 10	
Skiers			2 x 10	
Cable lift			2 x 8	
Medicine ball crunch throw			4 x 6	

Medicine ball throws supersetted with upper-body work

Lower-body work supersetted with plyometrics

RDL= Romanian dead lift   NSEW= North, south, east, west

STRENGTH SESSION 3

Exercise	Week 1	Week 2	Week 3	Week 4

STRENGTH SESSION 4

Exercise	Week 1	Week 2	Week 3	Week 4

RUNNING SESSION 1

Linear speed & aerobic endurance
- Dynamic warm-up
- Sprint drills (10 minutes)
- Acceleration runs (5 x 60 yards)
- Sprint-assisted runs (5 x 20 yards)
- Sprint-resisted runs (5 x 20 yards)

RUNNING SESSION 2

Agility
- Dynamic warm-up
- Agility technical drills (15 minutes)
- Sprint-assisted runs (4 x 20 yards)
- 4 x 30 yards (max speed)
- Open agility drills (20 minutes)

RUNNING SESSION 3

REGENERATION 1

Stretching session

REGENERATION 2

Pool session

Figure 14-10

selected are aimed at developing the ability to hold positions and produce movement—including explosive movement—in an unstable environment.

Medicine ball work is supersetted with upper-body exercises, with a total of 60 throws programmed. Plyometric work is supersetted with the lower-body exercises and includes 40 foot contacts of short-response drills and 40 foot contacts of long-response drills. These exercises all should be of maximum quality.

In-Season Week 4
(Figure 14-11)

Objective

The development of endurance is the primary focus of this week, with all other parameters on maintenance loads.

Resistance–Training Workouts

Exercises—Only the core exercises only are performed during this week.

Workout schedules—Routines utilize a twice-a-week schedule, with an emphasis on explosive and lower-body exercises during session 1 and an emphasis on upper-body exercises during session 2.

Loads—Loads are selected that target maximum strength or explosive power.

Sets/reps—A low number of sets (two or three) utilizing a low number of repetitions (three) are used as maintenance loads.

Exercise protocols and repetition cadence—All exercises are performed explosively.

Rest between sets—Rest between sets is long (three to five minutes or more) to allow for the use of maximal forces on subsequent sets.

Running Workouts

Speed and agility—Speed and agility work is limited to warm-ups and a low number of high-quality runs are performed to maintain the speed impulse.

Endurance—Three endurance sessions are carried out, each targeting one energy system (i.e., ATP-PCr, anaerobic glycolytic (lactic), and aerobic). In addition, the regeneration session involves a 40-minute Level 1 run. This session is the only time that long-distance running is used in this program.

Supplementary Work

Core-strength work is added to the second resistance-training session only.

TRAINING PHASE: IN-SEASON WEEK 4 | WEEKS 4 | EMPHASIS Endurance

MONDAY	TUESDAY	WEDNESDAY	THURSDAY	FRIDAY	SATURDAY	SUNDAY
Strength 1 (heavy lower body)	Regeneration 1	Strength 2 (heavy upper body)	Running 3	Regeneration 2	Game	Regeneration 2
Running 1 (pm)		Running 2				

STRENGTH SESSION 1

Exercise	Week 1	Week 2	Week 3	Week 4
Clean				3 x 3
Hang snatch				3 x 3
Squat				3 x 3
RDL				3 x 6

STRENGTH SESSION 2

Exercise	Week 1	Week 2	Week 3	Week 4
Bench press				2 x 8
Bent row				2 x 6
Upright row				2 x 6
Pikes				2 x 10
Skiers				2 x 10
Cable lift				1 x 8
Ramp				2 x 25 sec

STRENGTH SESSION 3

Exercise	Week 1	Week 2	Week 3	Week 4

STRENGTH SESSION 4

Exercise	Week 1	Week 2	Week 3	Week 4

RUNNING SESSION 1

Linear speed & aerobic endurance
• Dynamic warm-up
• Sprint drills (10 minutes)
• Acceleration runs (3 x 60 yards)
• 200-yard shuttle (6 reps, 2-minute recovery)

RUNNING SESSION 2

Agility & lactic endurance
• Dynamic warm-up
• Agility technical drills (15 minutes)
• 8 x 1 minute - level 5 endurance game 1:3 work/rest

RUNNING SESSION 3

PCr endurance
• Dynamic warm-up
• 2 x 5 x 60 yards (30-second recovery)

REGENERATION 1

40-minute run
Low intensity (50-60% MHR)
Stretching session

REGENERATION 2

Pool session

RDL = Romanian dead lift

Figure 14-11

In-Season Transition Cycles

(Figure 14-12)

Objective

Following two training cycles, a degree of fatigue will be present. The major aim at this point is to provide active recovery from the previous two cycles. This recovery takes the form of regeneration on a physiological and psychological basis.

Resistance-Training Workouts

The resistance-training workouts will be of a reduced volume (two per week). Session 1 will have a strength emphasis, but with a far lower volume than in the previous mesocycles. Session 2 will have an explosive emphasis and will be the lighter session of the week.

Running Workouts

No specific running workouts are programmed at this time. Instead, the athlete will be taking part in team practices, which will maintain the key fitness variables.

Regeneration

The stretching workouts have an important role in both facilitating regeneration and maintaining and developing the range of motion in key joints and muscle actions.

TRAINING PHASE: IN-SEASON TRANSITION				WEEKS 1		EMPHASIS	Active recovery
MONDAY	TUESDAY	WEDNESDAY	THURSDAY	FRIDAY	SATURDAY	SUNDAY	
Strength 1		Regeneration 1		Regeneration 2	Game	Regeneration 1	

STRENGTH SESSION 1

Exercise	Week 1	Week 2	Week 3	Week 4
Single-leg squat	2 x 8			
Hamstring lowers	2 x 8			
Incline dumbbell press	2 x 8			
Contralateral pull	2 x 8			
Reverse ramp	1 x 30 sec			
Side bridge	1 x 25 sec			
Cable lift	2 x 10			

STRENGTH SESSION 2

Exercise	Week 1	Week 2	Week 3	Week 4
Hang clean	2 x 4			
Hang snatch	2 x 4			

STRENGTH SESSION 3

Exercise	Week 1	Week 2	Week 3	Week 4

STRENGTH SESSION 4

Exercise	Week 1	Week 2	Week 3	Week 4

RUNNING SESSION 1

RUNNING SESSION 2

REGENERATION 1 — Pool workout

REGENERATION 2 — Stretching workout

Figure 14-12

In-Season Realization Cycle

(Figure 14-13 and 14-14)

Objective

This taper cycle runs over two weeks. It aims to reduce fatigue to a point where fitness gains are transmutated into optimal performance.

Resistance-Training Workouts

These workouts will be of a reduced volume, with three in the first week and one in the second. The emphasis moves from strength to explosive power. In week two, only explosive power is trained.

Running Workouts

Endurance is trained early in week one, followed by an emphasis on maximizing speed and agility utilizing high-quality work. Total volume is reduced through week 2.

Regeneration

Regeneration is stressed to maximize recovery and increase the likelihood of achieving optimal performance on the day of competition. The last three days before competition are totally devoted to regeneration.

TRAINING PHASE: IN-SEASON REALIZATION 1				WEEKS 1	EMPHASIS	Peak power & speed
MONDAY	TUESDAY	WEDNESDAY	THURSDAY	FRIDAY	SATURDAY	SUNDAY
Strength 1 (explosive & heavy lower body)	Strength 2 (heavy upper body) Running 1 (pm)	Running 2 (am) Regeneration 1 (pm)	Strength 3 (explosive & light total body)	Regeneration 2	Game	Regeneration 2

STRENGTH SESSION 1

Exercise	Week 1	Week 2	Week 3	Week 4
Power clean	3 x 3			
Snatch	3 x 3			
Squat	4 x 4			
RDL	3 x 3			
Calf raise	3 x 8			
Elbow crunches	2 x 10			
Reverse bridge	2 x 30 sec			
Skiers	2 x 10			
Cable chop	2 x 8			

Exercises supersetted with plyometrics

STRENGTH SESSION 2

Exercise	Week 1	Week 2	Week 3	Week 4
Bench press	3 x 4			
Bent row	3 x 4			
Shoulder press	3 x 4			
Pikes	2 x 10			
Log roll	2 x 10			
Cable lift	2 x 8			
Reverse ramp	2 x 30 sec			
Medicine ball crunch throw	4 x 4			

Upper-body exercises supersetted with medicine ball throws

RDL= Romanian dead lift

STRENGTH SESSION 3

Exercise	Week 1	Week 2	Week3	Week 4
Hang clean	3 x 3			
Squat	3 x 4			
Single-leg squat	2 x 5			
Glute hams	3 x 6			
Bench	3 x 4			
Contralateral pulls	3 x 4			

Lower-body exercises supersetted with plyometrics

All exercises performed explosively

STRENGTH SESSION 4

Exercise	Week 1	Week 2	Week3	Week 4

RUNNING SESSION 1

Linear speed & aerobic endurance
- Dynamic warm-up
- Sprint drills (10 minutes)
- Assisted sprints (4 x 20 meters)
- 4 x 40 yards (varied starts)
- 6 x 1 minute - level 5 endurance game 1:3 work/rest

RUNNING SESSION 2

Agility
- Dynamic warm-up
- Agility technical drills (15 minutes)
- Assisted runs (5 x 30 meters)
- Closed agility drills (5 minutes)
- Open agility drills (15 minutes)

RUNNING SESSION 3

REGENERATION 1

Stretching session

REGENERATION 2

Pool session

Figure 14-13

TRAINING PHASE: IN-SEASON REALIZATION 2

		WEEKS	2	EMPHASIS	Peak power & speed

MONDAY	TUESDAY	WEDNESDAY	THURSDAY	FRIDAY	SATURDAY	SUNDAY
Running 1	Strength 1	Running 2 (am) / Regeneration 1 (pm)	Regeneration 2	Regeneration 1	Game	Regeneration 2

STRENGTH SESSION 1

Exercise	Week 1	Week 2	Week 3	Week 4
Power cleans		3 x 3		
Hang snatch		3 x 3		
Plyometrics		50 foot contacts		
Medicine ball throws		30 throws		

STRENGTH SESSION 2

Exercise	Week 1	Week 2	Week 3	Week 4

STRENGTH SESSION 3

Exercise	Week 1	Week 2	Week 3	Week 4

STRENGTH SESSION 4

Exercise	Week 1	Week 2	Week 3	Week 4

RUNNING SESSION 1

Linear speed & aerobic endurance
- Dynamic warm-up
- Sprint drills (10 minutes)
- Acceleration runs (3 x 60 meters)
- Assisted runs (4 x 30 yards)
- 4 x 40 yards (varied starts)

RUNNING SESSION 2

Agility
- Dynamic warm-up
- Agility technical drills (15 minutes)
- Assisted runs (5 x 30 meters)
- Open agility drills (15 minutes)

RUNNING SESSION 3

REGENERATION 1

Stretching session

REGENERATION 2

Pool session

Figure 14-14

About the Author

Ian Jeffreys, B.A., M.Sc., CSCS*D, NSCA-CPT, ASCC, PGCE, is the director of athletics, sport science, and athletic performance at the Powys Sports Academy at Coleg Powys in Brecon, Wales. He is also the strength and conditioning advisor to the Welsh Rugby Union National Squad at Under 16 level.

Jeffreys is one of the leading strength and conditioning coaches in the UK, and through his company, All-Pro Performance, acts as a consultant to a number of athletes and teams. He is a director of the United Kingdom Strength and Conditioning Association (UKSCA). Jeffreys is also an accredited member of the UKSCA and an assessor for the UKSCA accreditation procedure. He is also a British Olympic Association registered strength and conditioning professional and a UK Athletics Level 3 Performance Coach for Sprints.

Jeffreys is a longstanding member of the National Strength and Conditioning Association (NSCA), where he is a Certified Strength and Conditioning Specialist, re-certified with distinction (CSCS*D). He is an NSCA coach practitioner and is also an NSCA-Certified Personal Trainer (NSCA-CPT), re-certified with distinction (NSCA-CPT*D). In 2006, he was voted NSCA High School Professional of the Year.

Jeffreys has authored a number of strength and conditioning articles and book chapters that have been featured in international publications. He has presented internationally in a range of strength and conditioning areas and delivers a strength and conditioning education program for the County of Powys.

Jeffreys lives in Brecon in Mid Wales, with his wife, Catherine, and son, James.